S0-EYQ-173

THE YEAR IN TENNIS 2003

DAVIS CUP by BNP PARIBAS

ITF

Text by Neil Harman

The International Tennis Federation

Universe

2003

the year in tennis

First published in the United States of America in 2004 by
UNIVERSE PUBLISHING A Division of Rizzoli International Publications, Inc.
300 Park Avenue South, New York, NY 10010

© 2003 The International Tennis Federation
Bank Lane, Roehampton, London SW15 5XZ, England

All rights reserved. No part of this publication may be reproduced, stored in a retrieval system, or transmitted in any form or by any means, electronic, mechanical, photocopying, recording, or otherwise, without prior consent of the publishers.

2004 2005 2006 / 10 9 8 7 6 5 4 3 2 1

ISBN: 0-7893-1069-4

Designed by Domino 4 Limited, Wimbledon, London

Printed in England

2003
the year in tennis

CONTENTS

4 President's message

6 Foreword by Lleyton Hewitt

8 Introduction

12 First Round

40 Profile: Ivan Ljubicic

42 Quarterfinals

60 Profile: Roger Federer

62 Semifinals

76 Profile: Carlos Moya

78 Play-off Round

96 Profile: Max Mirnyi

98 Final Round

116 Profile: Mark Philippoussis

118 Results

128 Acknowledgments and photography credits

PRESIDENT'S MESSAGE

IF ANYONE DOUBTS THE unique qualities of Davis Cup by BNP Paribas, one only needs to take a look at the 2003 final, in which Australia defeated Spain 3–1 in Melbourne to capture its twenty-eighth Davis Cup title.

All 45,000 tickets for Rod Laver Arena were sold out within half an hour of going on sale. Tennis Australia once again elected to transport a portable grass court to cover the permanent Rebound Ace surface. All four members of the winning team contributed a point toward Australia's triumph, the same team that Australia had fielded throughout the 2003 competition. And one member, Todd Woodbridge, became the most-capped Australian in Davis Cup history.

It is occasions such as these that continue to draw more fans to Davis Cup, which remains the largest annual international team competition in sport. In 2003, 135 nations took part in the event, either in the World Group or in one of three regional zones: Europe/Africa, the Americas, and Asia/Oceania. For teams such as Iceland, Panama, and Vietnam, winning promotion from Zone IV can be as significant as capturing the Davis Cup trophy itself.

Yet it is the support of the sport's leading players that remains the key to the success of Davis Cup. In 2003, eighteen of the world's top twenty were represented among the 569 competitors that contested the World Group and three regional zones. Their passion for the competition could be witnessed in scenes of jubilation at ties around the globe. Davis Cup final hero Mark Philippoussis called it the "best feeling I have ever had in my tennis career so far" and his sentiments have been echoed throughout the year.

The highlights of this year's competition have included Ivan Ljubicic's personal triumph against the United States; Switzerland's last-gasp victory against the Netherlands; Argentina's quarterfinal whitewash of defending champion Russia; Lleyton Hewitt's comeback against Roger Federer in the semifinals; and Australia's true team performance in the final.

Sports fans throughout the world will enjoy the in-depth look at all twenty-three World Group and play-off ties in the 2003 competition. My thanks go to our author, Neil Harman, who has now completed his fourth edition of the Davis Cup Yearbook. His research and attention to detail ensure that the book once again contains a comprehensive record of the Davis Cup year. Accompanying Neil's text are some wonderful photographs from the world's leading tennis photographers.

My congratulations go to Australia for its first title at home since 1986 and a place at the top of the ITF Davis Cup Nations Ranking. I must also recognize Spain's run through to the final, where it put up a brave fight against the home team. I would like to thank all 135 nations who took part this year and wish each nation well in their campaign for the 2004 Davis Cup by BNP Paribas.

Francesco Ricci Bitti
President, International Tennis Federation

2003

the year in tennis

5

2003

the year in tennis

6

FOREWORD

AS I WRITE THIS in December, 2003, I am reflecting back on a season of mixed results, but one that I can most certainly say ended for me with complete satisfaction.

While I may not have succeeded in my goal of winning a Grand Slam singles title for a third consecutive year, I am proud to say that I have accomplished my other major goal for the 2003 season: to help return the Davis Cup to Australia.

Indeed, that result gives me as much satisfaction as any of my achievements, tournament-wise, ranking-wise, or otherwise over the previous two years.

Some of those with less of an appreciation for Davis Cup and its place in our sport may wonder how a team competition played over four weeks throughout the year in various and sometimes odd locations around the globe could be comparable to the individual success enjoyed by winning your first Grand Slam title or your first Wimbledon. But that's never been my outlook.

Perhaps it was the values instilled in me by Newk and Roche when I first traveled to Davis Cup as an "orange boy", supporting them and my teammates in any way asked of me.

Perhaps it has something to do with the fact that the first tie I actually competed in was against the U.S. in Boston at the celebration of the 100th Anniversary of Davis Cup competition in 1999.

Perhaps it was the fact that I concluded that first season of Davis Cup play with a win on the road in Nice.

Perhaps it was our quarterfinal victory in Brazil in 2001, when I was able to clinch the tie with a win over Guga on clay in his hometown of Florianopolis in what many have said was one of my best performances ever.

Perhaps it was this season ... one in which some—not unfairly—judged my individual results as falling short of my potential, as I did not finish the year number one nor win a singles Grand Slam title, both of which I had achieved in each of the past two years.

But with wins this year over Thomas Enqvist in Sweden in the quarterfinal round, then down two sets to love and coming back to beat Wimbledon champ, Roger Federer, against the Swiss in the semis, and finally, defeating French Open winner, Juan Carlos Ferrero, to launch our victorious tie over Spain in the Final just last month, it shouldn't be hard to understand why there is no doubt that some of my greatest memories in tennis will be of this tremendous one-of-a-kind competition.

To the incredible Australian fans, both at home and those Fanatics and others who travel to support us around the globe, thanks so much for your extraordinary support on behalf of all of us once again this year. And to all of you tennis fans, regardless of nationality or allegiance, I hope you enjoy the words and photos here as much as I will for many years to come.

Lleyton Hewitt

INTRODUCTION

IT WAS 1946, THE Second World War was over, and the silver bowl of the Davis Cup with its distinctive weighty tray and even heavier base of wood and silver could safely be brought from its wartime safe haven of the vault of the Bank of New South Wales.

On December 26, 1946, it sat on the stadium court at Kooyong Tennis Club in Melbourne, shimmering in the blistering Australian heat. Standing next to it, his shoulders slightly rounded now, was Sir Norman "Wizard" Brookes, who had played fourteen ties for his country before the First World War. Brookes was waiting to address the sell-out crowd at the first Challenge Round since the end of the war and the death of the event's pioneer, Dwight Davis.

With famed hat in hand, the sixty-nine-year-old Brookes spoke with pride and emotion about knowing Davis, the great American entrepreneur and how the magnificent trophy that bore his name would be played for "as long as tennis retained its places in the hearts of young men who played in international competition."

Challenge Round matches in Australia were always at Christmastime, and Norman and Mabel Brookes would often entertain at their home with a huge holiday dinner for the team and other members of the tennis establishment. The Cup, brought out of the vault and prepared for its official appearances, would sit on the sideboard of the Brookes' dining room while guests happily chatted and relaxed in its company. Once, famously, Brookes' grandson, Norman, was seated at a table with Adrian Quist and Harry Hopman, Aussie legends both. While conversation took place around them, the three competed to see how many plastic counters each could flip into the bowl.

The tie in 1946 was, as it would be for the next thirteen years, between Australia and the United States. Ted Schroeder, fresh out of the US Navy, defeated John Bromwich in five sets in the first match, having lost the fourth set 6–0, playing hard enough to make Bromwich run but also conserving his own energies for the fifth. When Schroeder dashed for a drop shot at 5–3 in the fifth and clipped the ball just out of Bromwich's reach to win the match, he was afforded a five-minute standing ovation. As Nancy Kriplen in her absorbing book Dwight Davis: The Man and the Cup wrote eloquently: "If fine tennis and crowd good sportsmanship were indicators, the revived Davis Cup competition was off to the best possible start."

Jack Kramer won the second singles against Dinny Pails, and in the Saturday doubles, Kramer and Schroeder defeated Bromwich and Adrian Quist in straight sets. At the traditional dinner, Brookes said that Australia had got a first look at the "aggressive tennis which should have a great influence on our future stars and may in the long run help us to regain this coveted trophy."

In 1950, at Forest Hills, New York, after three further defeats to the United States, they did just that at the start of a remarkable run of success under Hopman, who took the captaincy of Davis Cup to a level unequalled before or since.

2003

the year in tennis

9

2003

the year in tennis

10

I was reminded of these flashbacks looking at the Davis Cup, perched on a couple more blocks of solid wood bearing hundreds more names and achievements. It was back shimmering in the sunshine of Melbourne during the 2003 World Group final between Australia and Spain, who, when Brookes spoke at Kooyong, was nineteen years away from making its first appearance in a final round, which would also, by a nice geographical quirk, be in Australia, at the Milton Courts in Brisbane, Queensland.

You could fill the Cup to overflowing with the blood, sweat, and tears that had been expended down the years as every subsequent young breed of player was entranced by the unique magic of the Davis Cup. As Australia marked the middle Saturday by bringing on to the Rod Laver Arena as many of their Davis Cup heroes as were well enough to make the journey, I looked at each one of them and wondered what marvelous tales they had to tell of the event and what it had meant in their lives.

Wouldn't Dwight Davis, watching over this from his heavenly perch, have a warm feeling as he saw how much it meant to generations so far removed from his own? It was written of Davis himself in 1903, in an article by the English brothers Reggie and Laurie Doherty that he "killed lobs harder than anyone else who has played the game."

And what was the final shot of the final a century later, but the killing of a lob from Juan Carlos Ferrero of Spain by Mark Philippoussis that nailed his place in the pantheon of the greats who have played for this majestic cup down the years.

Would not Brookes have loved to have Lleyton Hewitt around for dinner and a chat with the Cup on the sideboard? It is likely that Hewitt would not have been able to take his eyes off it. How many men out there would set out a stall at the beginning of a year to achieve one thing in their lives and end it with the task completed?

"Winning the Davis Cup, playing for your country, listening to the national anthem before ties—it's very hard to beat that. You have got this jacket on and it's something to be so proud of." Hewitt's captain, John Fitzgerald, spoke even more longingly about why the event has so held him in its thrall for years.

"I know there are kids who will have seen it (the final), and it will have been an inspiration for their future. It is tough to get numbers of kids into tennis in Australia, but I know the history and culture of the game in this country will continue to stand up. I want to be a part of what drives that. That is what these golden fleeces (the new jackets worn by his side) are. We believe in the sport and playing for Australia, and I know kids will be inspired by this. I just know it."

Not just in Australia, but everywhere. The magical effect of winning the Cup has lost nothing as the years have passed. Indeed, words written long ago have a resonance that is only enhanced with the passing of the mantle from one dynamic team to another. As Mabel Brookes noted in her fascinating autobiography Crowded Galleries: "There is something that brings savor to life as nothing else when, reading the international sports news, the man in the street puts down his paper and says "WE won the tennis, the little 'WE' automatically lifts the player involved into some sort of hierarchy. He belongs to his count, he has fought a battle, done a job for the people who now see themselves with him as one and indivisible."

These are sentiments that will resonate fully now with Mark Philippoussis, who won the decisive fourth rubber for the second time in his life to secure Australia their first victory on home soil in seventeen years. And this was two years after he was forced to hit balls from a wheelchair as he rehabilitated from a third knee operation that doctors feared would finish his career for good.

Philippoussis was proof—leaping, jumping, cavorting proof—of the extraordinary effect that this charismatic Cup has had on men down the years. It continues to span new horizons, forever casting a wider spell and drawing upon the richness of the human spirit to boldly go where one has never gone before. As Norman Brookes had said in the same city electrified by Philippoussis's performance fifty-seven years later, the Davis Cup will survive and prosper "as long as tennis retained its places in the hearts of young men who play in international competition."

Tennis would simply never be the same without it. ●

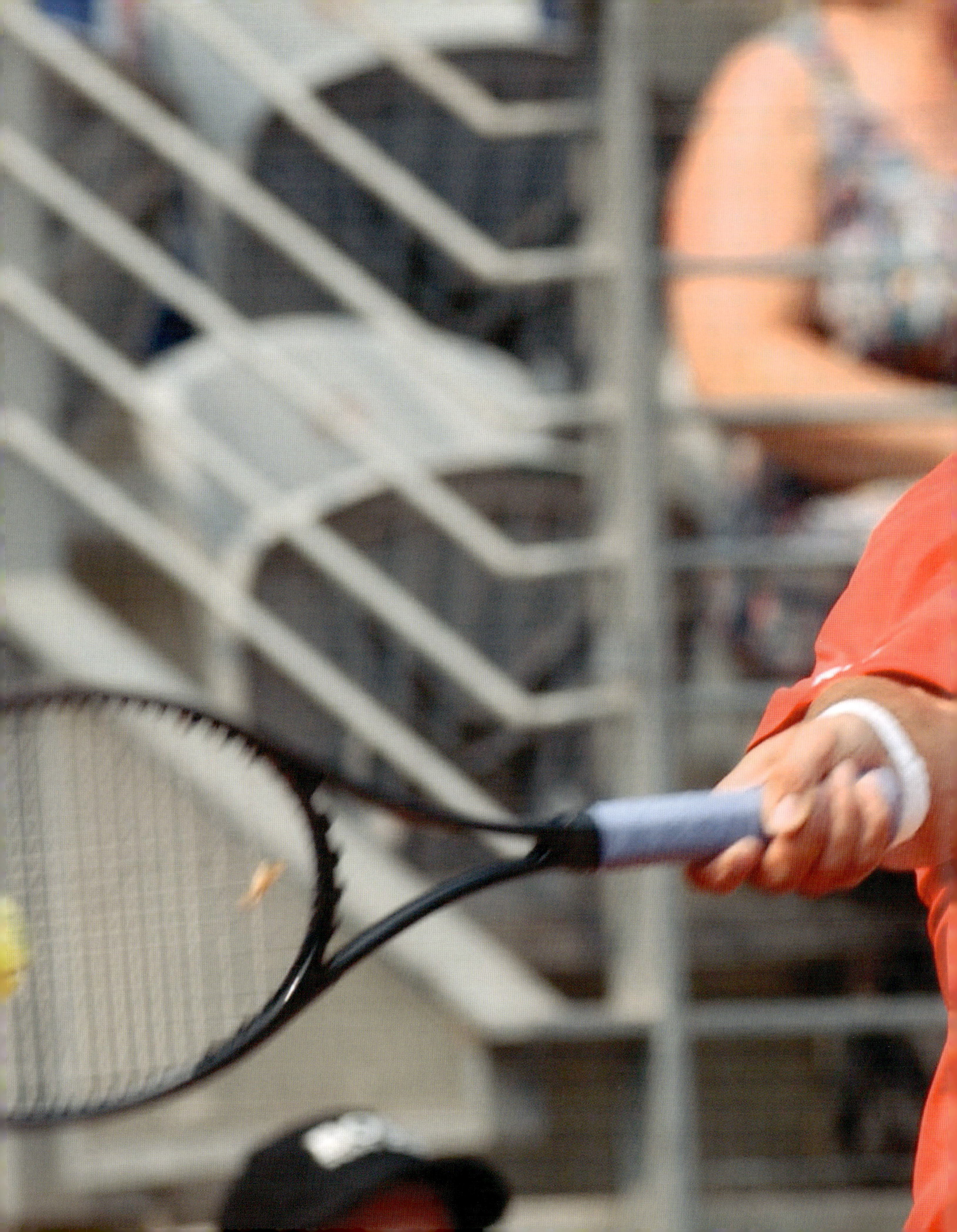

first round

France d. Romania 4–1   BUCHAREST, ROMANIA—INDOOR CARPET

Switzerland d. Netherlands 3–2   ARNHEM, NETHERLANDS—INDOOR CARPET

Australia d. Great Britain 4–1   SYDNEY, AUSTRALIA—OUTDOOR CLAY

Sweden d. Brazil 3–2   HELSINGBORG, SWEDEN—INDOOR CARPET

Croatia d. USA 4–1   ZAGREB, CROATIA—INDOOR CARPET

Spain d. Belgium 5–0   SEVILLE, SPAIN—OUTDOOR CLAY

Argentina d. Germany 5–0   BUENOS AIRES, ARGENTINA—OUTDOOR CLAY

Russia d. Czech Republic 3–2   OSTRAVA, CZECH REPUBLIC—INDOOR CLAY

FIRST ROUND

australia v great britain

14

FIRST ROUND

australia v great britain

AUSTRALIA v GREAT BRITAIN

WHEN IT WAS DECIDED that Great Britain would play Australia in the opening round of the 2003 Davis Cup by BNP Paribas, expectations of an exciting matchup between traditional rivals were high, with Lleyton Hewitt and Tim Henman serving as anchors for their respective teams. But Henman was recovering from surgery and unable to play. British captain Roger Taylor was forced to field a new-look team that introduced the name Boggo to Davis Cup. In the end, it was Australia that embarked on a journey that it hoped would lead all the way to the trophy itself.

Great Britain survived a whitewash only because Todd Woodbridge, who had turned up for the third day expecting to enhance his tan, was thrust into the world of singles from which he had all but retired. The Australian found himself confronted with a self-effacing teenager called Alex Bogdanovic, who wanted to prove something to himself.

Boggo, as he is nicknamed, defeated the old trooper 6–4, 7–6 to restore a sense of acceptability to the scoreline. He gave Taylor and the British LTA some reason to hope that there might be players in the country able to pick up the cudgels once Tim Henman could not rally to the cause anymore. Australia's march into the quarterfinals was due to its superior talent playing well enough to please the home crowd in Sydney.

There was a hint of surrealism about the tie from the moment Tennis Australia chose to play on a clay court purposely laid to counteract the strengths of the team it had expected to face: Henman and Greg Rusedski. They needn't have bothered as these two, plus the British number three, Martin Lee, were ruled out of contention through various injuries.

Tennis Australia's position was that New South Wales needed as many clay courts as it could lay its hands on, and that this was a means of impressing upon the state the importance of this particular surface in the teaching of the sport. More clay would, so the theory went, lead to more champions; Australia—despite having the number one player in the world in the men's game—was not exactly blessed with tremendous strength in depth.

Lucky for him, Australian captain John Fitzgerald did have Hewitt and Mark Philippoussis to spearhead his team, although he spent the two weeks leading up to the event denying that this was going to be an easy ride.

After a week watching his side practice, his counterpart Taylor declined to select the two more experienced players in his party, Arvind Parmar and Miles Maclagan—much to their dismay. The British captain plumped instead for Bogdanovic and Alan Mackin, who had spent a couple of years based at a clay-court academy in Monte Carlo, attempting to emulate the player he had admired above all others, Thomas Muster.

Mackin, all pale arms and legs, would require all of Muster's famed tenacity and self-belief when he was drawn to open the tie against Mark Philippoussis. The twenty-three-year-old Scot had never met anyone near the class of his opponent before, and when he

Pictured opposite:
Lleyton Hewitt (AUS)

Pictured left to right:
Great Britain's Davis Cup team;
Mark Philippoussis (AUS)

FIRST ROUND

australia v great britain

trailed 0–3 after only ten minutes, it was clear that there was a chance Britain might be heading for a huge embarrassment.

When Mackin slid forward to drive away a forehand volley on his first game point, he allowed himself a Hewitt-like "C'mon" to mark the confidence throbbing through his veins. The Scot then broke to bring the first set back to 4–3, but was undone in the next game, first by an overrule and then when he slid over trying to reach a forehand that wrong-footed him. Once he had pocketed the first set, Philippoussis was only intermittently disturbed en route to a 6–3, 6–3, 6–3 victory.

The introduction of Bogdanovic had long been anticipated by a British media corps keen to see how the left-hander, born in Belgrade, would handle a leap in class for him and a leap of faith by his captain. LTA officials in Sydney quizzed journalists to see if they felt Taylor was making the right decision and the answer was strongly in the affirmative. What was the point of taking him that far to leave him kicking his heels on the substitute's bench?

Bogdanovic did not flinch against Hewitt. Indeed, the first set turned into something of a classic contest between the world number one's nerveless attitude and a player who, from the outset, struck through the ball with commendable class and confidence. Hewitt did not quite know what to make of the kid—and neither did the English fans, who began to chant "Roger Taylor's Barmy Army" by way of replicating the antics of those who follow English cricket abroad.

Neither Bogdanovic nor Mackin ever really suggested one of them could win, but showed enough in terms of attitude and ability for the establishment to put the sackcloth and ashes back in the wardrobe. A teenage Tim Henman would have struggled to compete against someone of Hewitt's calibre as richly as Bogdanovic.

"I loved it out there," Bogdanovic said. "I started off a little bit nervous and he broke my first service game, but when I broke him straight back, I thought 'let's go.' I thought it was a good chance for me, and when I was up 4–2 and had him 0–30, I made a couple of small errors and that let him back. There is a long way for me still to go. I know I need to work on my physical fitness, but hopefully we shall see much more from me very soon."

Not only did Bogdanovic have to confront Hewitt but also a section of the stands at Homebush Bay housing the Aussie Fanatics. He had to be exceptionally well focused not to hear the exhortations "C'mon Lleyton, he's 450, you're the number one, wipe the floor with the Boggy boy," a reference to the commercial Hewitt has made promoting a particular brand of Aussie toilet paper. "And they kept shouting, 'Goran, Goran' at me," Bogdanovic said—hardly surprising given his service action is as exact a copy of 2001 Wimbledon champion Goran Ivanisevic as anyone has witnessed.

But everyone knew it was only a matter of time before Hewitt imposed himself. He was egged on by the crowd's antics and when he had finally gathered the first set 7–5, the second and third were relatively easy pickings.

Saturday's doubles brought the expected victory for Hewitt and Todd Woodbridge who defeated Parmar and Maclagan 6–1, 6–3, 4–6, 6–2, though, at least, the British pair prevented a nine-set whitewash. Although Wayne Arthurs defeated Maclagan in the first reverse singles, Bogdanovic's victory over Woodbridge in the final match sent the Brits home with hope for the future.

Australia was right to be confident of victory going into the tie. Captain John Fitzgerald said: "There is a special feeling about playing at home; we take whatever is dished up, but we love it here. I have a very committed team of guys." ●

Pictured left to right:
Australian fans;
Alex Bogdanovic (GBR)

FIRST ROUND
netherlands v switzerland

17

NETHERLANDS
v SWITZERLAND

FIRST ROUND

romania v france

20

FIRST ROUND

romania v france

ROMANIA v FRANCE

FRANCE BEGAN THE 2003 Davis Cup season ranked the best nation in the world in the ITF Nations Ranking. They had won the Cup in 2001 in compelling circumstances in Melbourne and lost it against Russia in Paris in December. Paul-Henri Mathieu, whose tears were captured so vividly in the pictorial reminiscences of that tie, had been unable to fully shake the despair from his body even months later.

Mathieu missed the Australian Open and was not considered fit enough to be a part of the team that faced an arduous trip to Bucharest. This is a city that has staged so many amazing ties in the past: Nastase and Tiriac contriving to lose against the USA in 1975, and a match staged within days of the fall of Ceausescu against Great Britain in 1989. Romania decided this time, rather than play on outdoor clay, to stage the tie on a carpet surface inside the Sala Polivalenta.

They say a wounded animal is a dangerous animal, an accurate representation of the French as they prepared for the tie. Sebastien Grosjean, for one, felt the defeat the previous year would serve merely to strengthen their noted camaraderie.

"It was really tough at the beginning and for the four or five days after," Grosjean said. "But I went back home to Florida with my wife, daughter, and son, thought about something else and tried to enjoy the 'real' part of my life. You learn more when you lose. When you win everything is fine, but when you lose you ask a lot of questions of yourself, and it is imperative to try to improve your game."

Considering France had featured in three finals in the past four years, the French understood the strategy and the commitment behind victory in this competition. But, despite all the French success, the twenty-four-year-old Grosjean did not underestimate the Romanians.

French captain Guy Forget was now in partnership with his new coach, Patrice Hagelauer, who had moved back from a spell in Great Britain. Together the pair continued to instill a unique sense of team spirit in their players, ensuring that they met up ten days in advance of each tie to prepare. The French were not huge stars in their own right, but their sense of togetherness, their esprit de corps, makes them almost unbeatable.

"Romania has good players," said Grosjean, "but we have good players too and we are really a team. In Davis Cup that can make the difference." Such a spirit was perfectly personified by the way every member of the side had comforted the twenty-one-year-old Mathieu, whose heartbreaking demise against Mikhail Youzhny from two sets up ultimately cost them the Davis Cup the previous year. The French side simply surrounded Mathieu and shared his pain.

Grosjean believes Mathieu has the guts and the game to come back stronger and better than before. "He is young, he has great potential, he won two tournaments in a row last year, and he's a really, really good player. He is going to

Pictured opposite:
Nicolas Escude (FRA)

Pictured left to right:
Sebastien Grosjean (FRA);
Adrian Voinea (ROM)

FIRST ROUND

romania v france

22

Pictured left to right:
Andrei Pavel (ROM);
The victorious French squad

learn a lot from that final, and he wants to come back and play a lot of Davis Cup matches."

Romania also fancied their chances. Although the participation of their number one man, Andrei Pavel, in the tie was questioned up to the last minute because of a lingering back injury, when it came to crunch time, he appeared on court to rapturous acclaim, with his country trailing 1–0. Grosjean had kept his word and played with such passion and commitment that Adrian Voinea had been unable to get close enough to threaten him in the opening singles.

Grosjean had been especially formidable on the forehand, the inside-out stroke from advantage court to opposite advantage court that is perhaps the best of the modern era. Voinea lost the first two sets in something of a blur, but came within two points of taking it to a fourth before Grosjean closed it out 6–2, 6–3, 7–6(10). Could Pavel turn the tide against Nicolas Escude? Initial signs were encouraging.

Pavel forced three break points in Escude's second service game but could not take advantage. There was not a further break point until the tiebreak. Pavel's back had only endured two matches this season but it seemed to be holding out, although he needed to win the tiebreak to have a chance. But it was Escude who skated it, racing in to a 5–1 lead and, on his first set point, cutting off a rather tame passing shot.

The second set confirmed France's domination. Escude broke in the opening game and the color drained from the Romanian's face. Though he managed one break point opportunity at 2–3, it was swiftly erased by an Escude ace, one of fourteen in the match.

Pavel decided to risk all on net-rushing, but the Frenchman wrapped up the second set 6–2.

At the beginning of the third set, the Romanian number one displayed his lack of concentration by going to the wrong side of the court. He realized his error when he saw Escude walk towards him, but recovered to hold serve.

As in the first rubber, the third set was the closest. Pavel raised his game and started to save face. Not a single break point was converted during the set, leading inexorably to another tiebreak. Once again the Frenchman was the quickest off the mark, taking his opponent's first service point. Escude held on to his mini-break, and when offered a match point at 6–5, a powerful backhand down the line applied the coup de grace.

"I am very proud of having won this match in three sets, without conceding a single break," said Escude. "The crowd was against us, yelling and singing, but that's Davis Cup, and that is what makes the beauty of this competition."

Romania had only once come back from a 0–2 deficit, in 1990 versus Ireland in a first round Zonal tie, and France was an altogether taller order. So it was that Michael Llodra and Fabrice Santoro, who had just lifted the Australian Open title, held firm against Pavel, willing to put his back through the exertion on a second day, and Gabriel Trifu. Their 6–4, 6–3, 7–6(4) victory ensured that the 2002 finalists had reached the quarterfinals without dropping a set, conceding only a single break of serve. ●

FIRST ROUND

sweden v brazil

23

SWEDEN
v BRAZIL

FIRST ROUND

argentina v germany

26

FIRST ROUND

argentina v germany

ARGENTINA v GERMANY

BEFORE JANUARY, RAINER SCHUETTLER had a reputation as a decent tennis player who had won a couple of tournaments. People knew that he was blessed with a superb physique but felt he would never make it on the really big stage. They were proved wrong when he reached the final in Melbourne in January. The tournament whose record book was becoming a repository for tennis's lesser lights added Schuettler to its list in 2003, a list that included 2002 champion Thomas Johansson and 2001 finalist Arnaud Clement.

And though he had been gobbled up by Andre Agassi on the last day in Melbourne and arrived in Buenos Aires for the tie against Argentina with his tail somewhat between his legs, there was genuine hope in the German camp that Schuettler might rouse himself to Melbourne levels.

How Germany needed him. The new captain, Patrik Kuhnen, knew Tommy Haas would be a long-term absentee because of troubles with his shoulder, though he offered moral support by flying to South America from his home in Florida. In addition, Nicolas Kiefer was in another of his deep and debilitating struggles for form. So the hopes of the nation rested firmly on Schuettler's shoulders.

From the searing heat of Melbourne, where temperatures had fallen only slightly from the record high of forty-four Celsius on women's final day, it seemed a bit of a blessing when the Germans stepped off the plane into cool, windy conditions in the Argentine capital.

Schuettler did not have much time to acclimatize. The draw would pitch him headlong into the first rubber, against fast-rising Gaston Gaudio, who had finished 2002 ranked twenty-one in the world, twelve places ahead of the German number one.

In truth, Schuettler hardly got out of the blocks. Such was Gaudio's electric form and speed across the court, giving him opportunity time and again to unwrap his flowing single-handed backhand, that his opponent managed a mere five games in three sets, losing 6–2, 6–3, 6–0.

Schuettler was bamboozled, and no exhortations from Kuhnen could make the slightest difference. It is unlikely Gaudio had ever played a better match in more appropriate circumstances, and the 1–0 lead from his performance was soon to be enhanced by David Nalbandian's powerful performance against Lars Burgsmuller. Nalbandian, the youngest and highest-ranked player of the tie, was expected to win, but that does not always follow, as Davis Cup historians will quickly tell you.

Under the cover of cloudy skies and with the aid of a brisk wind, an eight-thousand-strong Buenos Aires crowd was determined not to let disappointing weather dampen spirits. The first set started much the same way as the first singles, with Burgsmuller finding it difficult to settle into any rhythm in the blustery conditions. Nalbandian was by far the more composed of the two and, like his teammate, settled quickly, breaking the Burgsmuller serve in the opening game.

Pictured opposite:
Gaston Gaudio (ARG)

Pictured above:
David Nalbandian and Lucas Arnold (ARG)

FIRST ROUND

argentina v germany

The German's serve, with its very distinctive high-ball toss, could be vulnerable at the best of times, and in a blustery, capricious wind he struggled for consistency. Through the course of the match he struck twelve double-faults and was broken seven times. In contrast, a relaxed Nalbandian struck an impressive 71 percent of first serves, broke serve four times, and won twenty-nine of the forty-seven points in the opening set.

The second set was much more like a traditional clay-court match, with both players rallying hard from the back of the court. The grueling tiebreak went the way of the Argentine, despite more aggression from his opponent.

By the beginning of the third set, not only had the sun emerged from behind the clouds, but the tennis had also reached a decent level with both men playing at the top of their game. Burgsmuller's shotmaking became increasingly daring with a number of successful approaches to the net. The German managed to mix his game up well and disrupt Nalbandian's rhythm by employing a variety of chip-charges, lobs, and drop shots.

True to his greater exposure to bigger matches, Nalbandian was solid enough to withstand the fight back and held on to win 6–1, 7–6(4), 7–5. To have held a player ranked sixty-four places above him for as long as he did meant Burgsmuller could reflect positively: "It was my first experience of Davis Cup and is certainly the largest crowd I have played in front of. I was very nervous at the start, especially with the noise the crowd was making. Despite losing, I am happy."

Another doubles, another five-setter. And what a fluctuating, fascinating match it was, as Nalbandian and Lucas Arnold took on Schuettler and another debutant, Michael Kohlmann. The first two sets set the trend, the Argentines winning the first 6–1 and losing the second 6–0.

A bewildered crowd wondered what would happen next but did not expect the Germans to edge ahead, as the inexperienced Kohlmann put himself through every emotion to try to wrest the initiative back for his country. It took its toll. Though the Germans won the third set, Kohlmann required an injury time-out at the start of the fourth and their rhythm was fatally disrupted.

The Argentine side drew breath, composed themselves, and forged through, losing only three games in the final two sets to win 6–1, 0–6, 4–6, 6–1, 6–2. The tie was conclusively theirs.

The margin of victory became 5–0, thanks to victories for Juan Ignacio Chela and Gaudio on the last day. That only served to emphasise the remarkable strength in depth of a team that had Guillermo Canas coming back after injury and that could afford to leave Guillermo Coria, on the verge of a top-twenty ranking, on the sidelines.

Captain Gustavo Luza was properly proud. "I am very happy that Argentina has very few limits at the moment," he said. "I think that if it (Davis Cup victory) doesn't come this year, then it's going to be soon. If all of the six or seven players on the squad really believe in themselves, then I think Argentina can win anywhere and against anyone. It's up to them and it's up to me to convince them.

"I feel very confident about the next round (against title-holder Russia). I believe in my players. I believe in our performance. We are very strong here in Buenos Aires because of the clay and this noisy crowd. Whoever comes here will have to be very strong to beat us." ●

Pictured left to right:
German captain Patrick Kuhnen and Rainer Schuettler;
Lars Burgsmuller (GER)

Pictured opposite:
David Nalbandian (ARG)

FIRST ROUND

argentina v germany

29

FIRST ROUND
czech republic v russia

30

FIRST ROUND

czech republic v russia

CZECH REPUBLIC v RUSSIA

WHEN THE FINAL MATCH of the tie extended to the fifth and decisive rubber, it is likely that Robert Krechler, captain of the Czech Republic, had a queasy feeling in the pit of his stomach. Of their five losses in Davis Cup ties in the previous five years, each one had been in the fifth and last match. Was heartbreak to strike again for the Czechs, still clinging miraculously to their place in the World Group?

It is not as though Radek Stepanek or Nikolay Davydenko, the two men who would take part in this fascinating denouement, had much of a Davis Cup heritage. Indeed, this was the first tie for both men, so what had happened in the past meant next to nothing. Both, though, were aware of the depth of the responsibility.

Russia was the Davis Cup champion nation, having defeated France 3–2 last December. The memory of those magical moments in Paris was still ferociously bright, even for Davydenko, who hadn't been there in person but watched with wonder as compatriot Mikael Youzhny came through from two sets down in the most exhilarating fashion, in the fifth against Paul-Henri Mathieu of France. Now it was his opportunity, and though Ostrava's Palac Kultury Sportu was a million leagues away from the pomp and circumstance of the Palais Omnisports de Bercy, a job was a job.

These were the moments for which Davydenko had trained so hard, having moved from a small tennis club in Severodonezk, in the Ukraine, via Volgograd in Russia to Salmtal in Germany, where he now lives. He would find it hard to come to terms with being a new Russian hero. But that was what he was to become in a wondrous exposition of the trials and tribulations of Davis Cup tennis.

While the venue may have been different, the final match of the tie proved to be a stirring reminder of Russia's victory in Paris as Davydenko defeated Stepanek 1–6, 7–6(4), 6–2, 3–6, 6–0 to seal the victory. He understood that he had accomplished something that would stay with him forever.

"I am very happy, because this is one of the biggest days of my career. The tie was broadcast to Russia, so now everybody at home knows not only Safin, Kafelnikov, and Youzhny, but also me," Davydenko said, smiling. It was only the second five-set match of his career, and the first he had won. "But it was so hard, not only physically but psychologically. I knew that if I lose, my team loses, too."

It was the Czech player who had a dream start. Serving and moving well on the clay, Stepanek didn't give his opponent many chances in the first set. But Davydenko was patient. He gradually played more aggressively, started to serve well, and his forehand was his killer shot. "I was a little bit nervous before the match, but not when I stepped on the court," Davydenko said. "I was just surprised how well Stepanek played in the first set."

After losing the second and third sets, Stepanek started to play more aggressively, carving a 4–1 lead in the fourth set, and with the support of five thousand noisy fans behind him, he won the set, making Davydenko run with his use of

Pictured opposite:
Nikolay Davydenko (RUS)

Pictured left to right:
Mikhail Youzhny (RUS);
Jiri Novak (CZE)

F FIRST ROUND

c spain v belgium

36

FIRST ROUND

spain v belgium

SPAIN v BELGIUM

THERE WAS NOT A player in the sport's rarefied echelons that entered 2003 with more to prove—both to himself and a rather skeptical world—than Juan Carlos Ferrero. Twice a semifinalist at Roland Garros, he had taken his career a step further by reaching the 2002 final, only for the ankle injury he had carried since the second round to take its toll.

Ferrero required an astonishing forty-five injections for pain during the French Open, and it caught up with him when he wanted to be fresh against Albert Costa. The French team doctor said if one of his players had been in a similar position, he would not have countenanced administering such huge doses of anaesthetic.

The final of the Tennis Masters Cup in Shanghai in November was equally soul-destroying for Ferrero, who had won the first two sets against Lleyton Hewitt and was 3–1 ahead in the fifth when the Australian staged another remarkable comeback.

But if those two memories were unpleasant to conjure, Ferrero could always remind himself of his performance in the 2000 Davis Cup Final when he was raised up before the Spanish king after leading his country to the crown for the first time. And it was a new year and a new opportunity for Spain in Davis Cup. This year's first round tie against Belgium should not present the current team (which, with the exception of Juan Balcells, was exactly the same as the championship team) with an insurmountable task, with hope that Spain would go all the way again.

For the first time in eleven years, a Davis Cup team featured three players from the world's top ten: Ferrero (three), Carlos Moya (four), and Costa (eight). A home tie in Seville on clay against this juggernaut of a team gave some idea of the challenge confronting an overachiever of a country like Belgium that had done well to hold onto its World Group status for so long. And then came the most intriguing element of the team selection, when Belgian captain Steve Martens decided to play Christophe Rochus ahead of his younger but higher-ranked brother, Olivier, for the opening singles.

The choice astounded the Belgian followers, but there had been many occasions in the competition's diverse history where inspired choices came good. This was not to be one of those, as Ferrero, lean, mean, and so solid from the back of the court, dusted his opponent for the loss of a mere five games in the first two sets.

Rochus, to be fair to him, staged a recovery in the third, holding a point to take the rubber into a fourth set, but Ferrero regained his poise and saw Spain to a 1–0 lead with a 6–3, 6–2, 7–5 victory.

Then, of all things in the south of Spain, it decided to rain, and rain hard. A near two-hour delay resulted in a scrappy start between Moya and Xavier Malisse, who had contributed so mightily to Belgium's rise up the tennis ranks in the past couple of years. But Moya, who was not included in the Spanish team that won the Cup in 2000, was a man with a mission. Malisse may have taken him to a couple of

Pictured opposite:
Carlos Moya (ESP)

Pictured left to right:
Xavier Malisse (BEL); Spanish fans

FIRST ROUND

spain v belgium

Pictured left to right:
Christophe Rochus (BEL);
Juan Carlos Ferrero (ESP)

Pictured opposite:
Alex Corretja and Albert Costa (ESP)

tiebreaks, but Moya's greater consistency earned its reward, 7–6(2), 6–1, 7–6(5).

That left the recalled Olivier Rochus and Kristof Vliegen to try to keep Belgium's heads above water. It would not be easy against the best friends and Olympic bronze medalists, Alex Corretja and Albert Costa. It proved to be the match of the tie. Not only did the Belgians recover from two sets to one down to lead 2–0 and 5–4 in the decisive fifth set, they silenced a Spaniard crowd in the process, which is no small feat.

The Spanish supporters had crammed into the newly built Olympic tennis facility in the Andalusian capital and it needed all of their considerable vocal talents to keep Costa and Corretja in a dramatic match. The tall, pipe-reed thin Vliegen and the diminutive Rochus made for an odd couple on court, but they soon showed they could pose serious problems for the Spaniards as they broke the first Corretja service game.

Spain hit straight back, and after another exchange of breaks it was the home team who edged ahead, Corretja becoming the first player to hold his serve in game five after coming through six deuces. Spain built on that narrow advantage and pocketed the first set 6–4. Then Corretja was broken early in the second, and this time the Belgians consolidated their advantage. They were all square after forty-nine minutes.

After the Spanish pair captured the third set, it was extraordinary to see them fall away so rapidly in the fourth, where Rochus and Vliegen led 5–0. A brief revival could not prevent a second comeback and a decisive fifth set was required.

A Belgian win was in sight as Vliegen produced a booming return of the Corretja serve to set up break point for a 5–4 lead. Vliegen couldn't take his chances when serving for the match, however, and the Belgians paid the price for that missed opportunity. Rochus did manage to hold in game twelve, but Vliegen once again failed on his next service game as the match entered its fifth hour.

Costa hit a sublime winner down the line to set up match point, and a tired Rochus netted an easy volley to hand the match to Spain 6–4, 4–6, 6–3, 3–6, 8–6.

The acclaim was raucous. Corretja and Costa lifted each other's arms and cruised the court. On the dead rubber day, Ferrero accounted for Vliegen for the loss of five games and Moya for Christophe Rochus, losing only four. It was (the doubles outstandingly apart) a pretty one-sided 5–0 victory. Then the Spaniards—who have christened this year Reconquista—learned that they would be facing Croatia at home in the quarterfinals.

"They have two big servers, but on a clay court we should be able to counter that tactic," a confident Ferrero said. "We'll put up a great wall to stop them." It promised to be quite a prospect. ●

FIRST ROUND

spain v belgium

39

FIRST ROUND
ivan ljubicic

PROFILE

Name IVAN LJUBICIC

Born MARCH 19, 1979, IN BANJA LUKA, BOSNIA-HERZEGOVINA

Turned Professional 1998

Davis Cup Records SINGLES 10-9 DOUBLES 7-4

AT THE ITALIAN OPEN in May, Ivan Ljubicic walked into a press conference as the home writers were preparing to warmly greet one of their own, Filippo Volandri. There was a strained silence as the journalists rustled their papers and wondered what the Croat's result had been, whom he played next, and what the heck they could possibly ask him.

The usual clearing of throats and the innocuous "So how did it go today Ivan" followed. He answered in English and just as the interpreter readied herself to answer in the home language, he stopped her and gave an answer in such wonderfully fluent Italian, the socks were completely knocked off the audience. He then kept them enthralled for fifteen minutes until they had completely forgotten who was next.

That is Ljubicic, not only a wonderful talent but a man of enormous intelligence, fun, and dexterity. He had to come by all of this the hard way. Ljubicic's home is Banja Luka, in Bosnia-Herzegovina, a place that became infamous for atrocities during the Balkan War of the 1990s. Ljubicic was thirteen and was becoming fascinated by tennis, but he knew also that things were not good, simply because he was a Croat in the wrong place at the wrong time.

"One day, a family you knew was there, the next they were gone," he said. "It was frightening. My parents were worried. My mother is Muslim and my father decided that she, my older brother, and I would leave. We got the last plane out at that time to Belgrade. Then we had a twenty-four-hour bus ride to Opatija in Croatia. The whole trip took three days but at least now we were in a safe place."

Ljubicic, mother Hazira, and brother Vlado were assigned to a refugee camp, an old hotel for six months. Father Marko was still missing. "We didn't have word from him for the longest time, but he had escaped and we managed to get together in Rijeka, where we have an apartment."

It was from there that Ljubicic escaped again, but this time for the sake of his sport. "I couldn't develop in Croatia and there was a chance to move to Italy, offered by a club that wanted to help out kids from the war zone." It was Ljubicic's great fortune to be put in touch with an excellent and caring coach in Como, Riccardo Piatti. They have been together since.

He has been called the man with the unpronounceable name (Loo-bee-chich) and the unapproachable serve. He is feted now in Croatia, where the country knew in 2003 that Goran Ivanisevic was winding down. Ljubicic remembers the day Ivanisevic won Wimbledon as if it was yesterday.

"I was in Gstaad, ready to go out and play a match. I watched the final on TV and went out with tears streaming down my face. I went out and beat Roger Federer two and one. Nothing was going to stop me that day." With what he has had to put up with in his life, it is no wonder Ivan Ljubicic finds tennis the ultimate release. ●

FIRST ROUND

ivan ljubicic

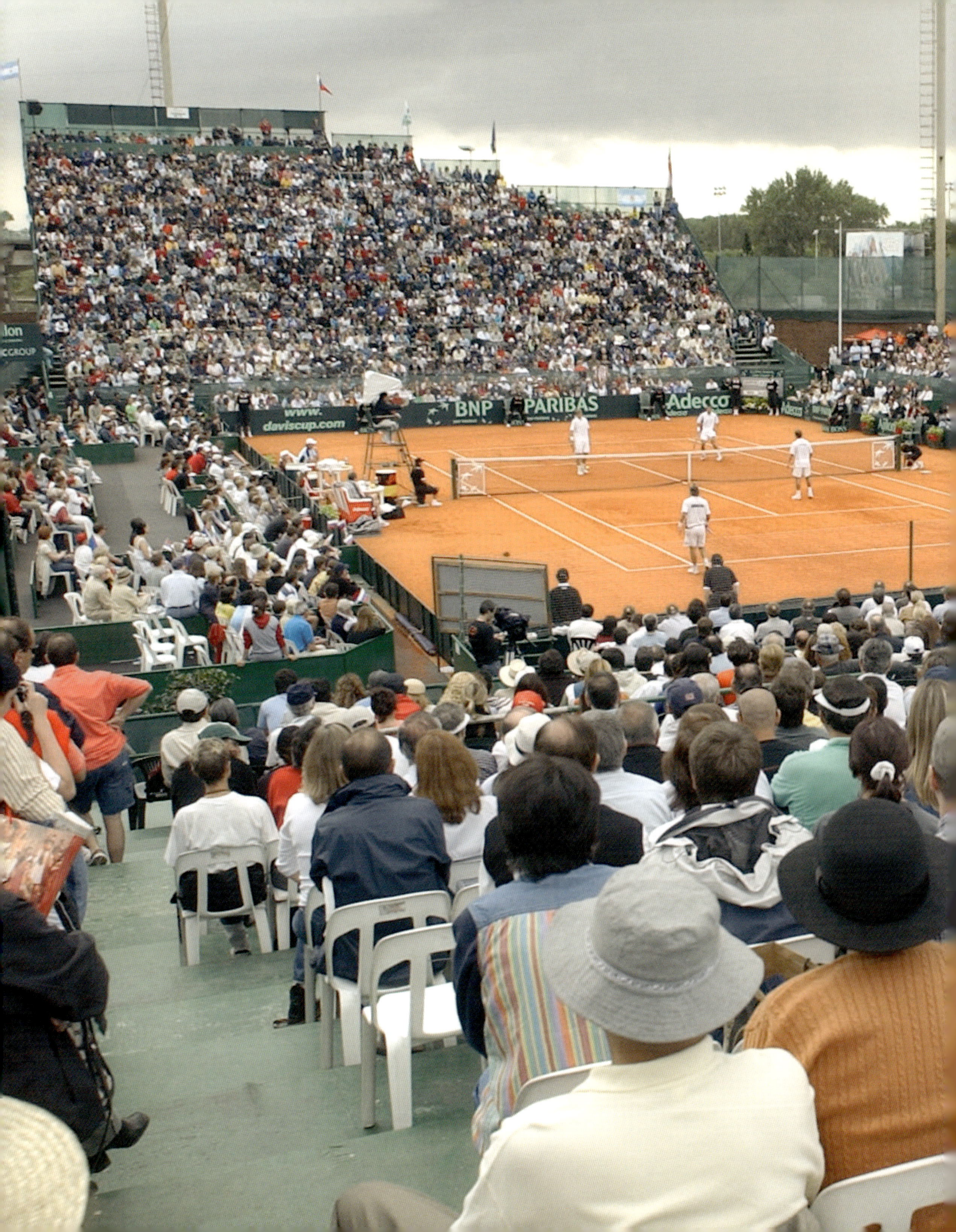
www.
daviscup.com
BNP PARIBAS
Adecco

quarterfinals

Switzerland d. France 3-2 TOULOUSE, FRANCE—INDOOR HARD
Australia d. Sweden 5-0 MALMO, SWEDEN—INDOOR HARD
Spain d. Croatia 5-0 VALENCIA, SPAIN—OUTDOOR CLAY
Argentina d. Russia 5-0 BUENOS AIRES, ARGENTINA—OUTDOOR CLAY

QUARTERFINALS

sweden v australia

44

QUARTERFINALS

sweden v australia

SWEDEN v AUSTRALIA

FENTON COULL, THE MISTER FIX-IT of Tennis Australia, was pleased with life. Australia had won their Davis Cup by BNP Paribas first round tie; Brazil was, it seemed, home and dry against Sweden; and he had already located the site for their quarterfinal home tie. Even as the Australian team was walking off court in Sydney after their first round triumph over Great Britain, the announcement was made to the crowd to get ready for Perth in April. Then Jonas Bjorkman and Andreas Vinciguerra intervened. Coull's best-laid plans had to be ripped up.

Rather than traveling to Western Australia, the Aussies would be heading for Western Europe. Sweden had produced an almighty victory, and John Fitzgerald's team, contemplating a four-hour flight to Perth, would instead be undertaking a twenty-four-hour journey to Malmö, via London and Copenhagen. Such were the wondrous vagaries of the competition.

The rehabilitation of Mark Philippoussis had begun convincingly in Sydney and would be continued against the Swedes. Lleyton Hewitt had won the singles titles in Scottsdale and Indian Wells but had slid to an unexpected defeat in Key Biscayne, perhaps from playing too much. Even an athlete as brilliant as he needed time to settle the body.

He arrived in Sweden quite prepared to shoulder the mantle of Australia's load but certain that, in harness with Philippoussis, Australia would win and move closer to Davis Cup glory in 2003. And it was exactly the kind of surroundings in which he reveled: a tight, sardine-tin of a venue, a raucous crowd, most bedecked in the colors of the opposition, and so much of the onus on him.

In the first rubber, Philippoussis managed to contain the energy and drive of Jonas Bjorkman. Indeed, there was a poise and purpose about the big man who hadn't been seen in Australian colors for a good few years. His 6–4, 6–3, 6–3 victory was all hustle and bustle: emphatic service games, power off the ground, and a refusal to be sidetracked by Bjorkman's attempts to pump up both himself and the crowd.

All observers at the Baltiska Hallen agreed that this was Philippoussis at his mighty best. Hewitt was entranced by it, as was captain John Fitzgerald, who said, "Mark played almost faultless tennis. He is playing as well as he has in three years. If he stays healthy, he is going to give the world of tennis a bit of a shake."

Hewitt had already managed to do just that. He had shaken Thomas Enqvist in five of their previous six meetings on the tour, and it was no wonder he appeared cool and composed stepping into the breach. "Certainly Flip's win was a good thing to have on my mind," he said later. "He had destroyed Jonas, taking away all his weapons. So Thomas must have known he'd had to do something special."

He had changed his hairstyle, which was a start. Enqvist sported a modified Mohawk, perhaps in an attempt to intimidate his opponent. He was the only player in 2003 to have beaten Andre Agassi, so there was that inspiration

Pictured opposite:
Mark Philippoussis (AUS)

Pictured left to right:
Lleyton Hewitt (AUS);
Todd Woodbridge and
Wayne Arthurs (AUS)

QUARTERFINALS

sweden v australia

upon which to draw. And Enqvist had good reason to remember Malmö fondly as the site of the 1996 Davis Cup Final when he won two critical matches.

Although he was not broken early in the match against Hewitt, it was clear that the Enqvist serve was going to be crucial. In the fifth game, the Swede saved the first break point with a towering ace and then required two more to extricate himself in his next service game. The tide was already turning the way of the green and gold.

The entourage was in place. Hewitt's parents, Glynn and Cherilyn, sister Jaslyn, and Lleyton's girfriend, Belgian superstar Kim Clijsters, were pumping their man up, and it was no surprise that Hewitt closed out the first set 6–4. Swift and strong and full of flash, Australia's number one looked set to turn in his nineteenth Davis Cup singles victory, and he soon wrapped up the second set 6–2.

Enqvist had a lot more fire in his belly at the start of the third, and snatched the initiative for the first time in the sixth game. Sparked, Hewitt broke back and tied the set up at 4–4. Serving at 5–6, Hewitt again struggled and this time was unable to salvage the game or the set as Enqvist, with a firm forehand volley crosscourt, converted his second set point to take it 7–5. He leapt into the embrace of his captain, Mats Wilander.

The momentum didn't last long. Hewitt was soon back to his scrapping best, and at 4–4 came the tie's decisive moment, with the Swede facing three break points. Hewitt only needed one, scrambling and hitting a backhand near-winner that Enqvist scuffed into the net. Serving for the match, the Aussie played another brilliant game. How often had we seen that before?

"We realized we had to play at the highest level to beat Lleyton and Mark," said the Swedish captain. "Mark played unbelievably well, and Lleyton has played well all year in every match. Thomas hits the ball better, but that's not all you have to do to beat Lleyton."

The Aussies might have subdued the team, but they did not subdue the spirit of the Swedish players or fans whose love of Davis Cup is legendary and whose reputation as the comeback kids in this competition is well known, having survived a 0–2 deficit five times in history.

Hewitt worried not. "I played well from the start today, and then it turned into a dog fight," he said after his 6–4, 6–2, 5–7, 6–4 victory. "Thomas played as well as anyone can play, but I raised the bar. The last two games were two of the best I've ever played in my career."

The tie was to be settled the next afternoon in glorious style. Todd Woodbridge and Wayne Arthurs played the doubles of their dreams to defeat Bjorkman and Enqvist 6–4, 6–2, 6–2 in an hour and forty-five minutes. And yet, at the outset, it looked as if the crowd could be in for a long Saturday at the tennis movies.

Bjorkman held serve in the opening game, but Arthurs faced three break points in the next game. Trailing 0–40, the lefthander unleashed three aces, two on consecutive points, which relaxed him to play the finest doubles of his life. He knew that Woodbridge would be fine. From the outset, the man who had won seventy-four doubles titles in his career was on the button, consistently splitting the opposition down the middle.

"It was just outstanding the way they both played and the way they combined," said Fitzgerald. "I thought it was by far and away the best doubles match they have played for Australia and also by far and away the best these two guys have played together."

Even though the Australians broke Bjorkman's serve three times, they concentrated their attack on Enqvist, and it worked. The Swedes could not penetrate a defense that was as tough as Aussie boot leather. Even when Arthurs was floored by a direct hit to the stomach, it did not mar the flow of excellence from their side.

"I can't believe how it has all gone for me," said Arthurs. "I am thirty-two and probably playing the best tennis ever. I played some good doubles matches leading up to this tie so I felt a little bit confident. I have really practiced very well and didn't get on myself, and stayed calm."

The win was extra special for Woodbridge, who has now won twenty-one Davis Cup doubles matches, making him the leading player for Australia in Davis Cup doubles. "I was unaware going into today's match that I could break that record," he said. "Honestly, I never expected to do that. To play this long and be that successful, be it in doubles or whatever, it's more than I expected. It was my dream to play Davis Cup, but to do as well as I have is beyond anything I dreamt about."

Fenton Coull was smiling too. This time he did have a home tie to prepare for. Just one round later than he had anticipated.

Pictured opposite:
Jonas Bjorkman (SWE)

QUARTERFINALS

sweden v australia

47

QUARTERFINALS
spain v croatia

48

QUARTERFINALS
spain v croatia

SPAIN v CROATIA

THEIR DARING DEEDS AGAINST the United States had made the men from Croatia feel different about themselves. Even though Goran Ivanisevic would not be in Spain, they could draw on the part he played in the first round for inspiration so that the trip to Valencia need not be tagged in the impossible category. But they knew it would be tough.

Ivan Ljubicic described it as "the worst draw. They have the number three, four, seven, and fifteen in the world and all of them have played in the final of Roland Garros. Two of them, (Carlos) Moya and (Albert) Costa, have won it. We are talking about the best on their favorite surface." Truly, if Croatia emerged with a place in the last four, it would rank foremost among the most remarkable performances of the past decade.

They knew they would have few friends in the ten-thousand-seat Tennis Club de Valencia stadium in the south of Spain. And Ljubicic wondered whether it might be all too much for his young colleague Mario Ancic. Drawing on his own experience, he knew how much the burden of carrying the Croatian colors abroad could affect a teenager.

"In 1997, when Goran decided not to play Davis Cup for the first time, I became the number one player at nineteen and it was a terrible experience," he said.

"I had so many ups and downs. For those three years without Goran, it was difficult, especially for the spirit and the atmosphere in the team. When he came back, we were in the Euro/African Zone II, and it takes time to get back into the World Group. Now we have managed it; we want to try to stay there."

But Ivanisevic's girlfriend was nearly eight months pregnant with their first child and Goran did not want to leave her side so close to the expected birth. He had cut his foot badly on a jagged piece of glass while on a beach in Miami and though one half of him wanted to be in Valencia to help his side along, if only by screaming at them, he decided to remain at home in Split.

As soon as Ivanisevic's foot was diagnosed worse than he had first feared, the Croats knew they would be offering Ancic alongside Ljubicic in the singles, and the signs were not beneficial. Poor Ancic was a frightening mess in practice, barely winning a game, let alone a set. A sinking feeling overcame Ljubicic. "We knew clay was not Mario's chosen surface, but we could not do anything else," he said.

As it was, Ancic drew on the occasion against the Spanish number one, Juan Carlos Ferrero, and gave a spirited account of himself. Perhaps he had heard of Ancic's troubles in practice, for Ferrero was surprisingly hesitant at the outset, as if unsure what to expect. He missed one chance for an early break in the first set, over-hitting a backhand after forcing the opportunity with a stinging return to his opponent's feet. The breakthrough eventually came in the ninth game and, with it, the set 6–4.

The first two games of the second set saw the contest slip away from Ancic. Ferrero broke his opponent to love before saving six break points in a game that went to seven

Pictured opposite:
Alex Corretja (ESP)

Pictured left to right:
Juan Carlos Ferrero (ESP);
Albert Costa (ESP)

QUARTERFINALS

spain v croatia

deuces. Building on that escape, the Spaniard took the second set 6-2 in forty-two minutes.

Ancic showed great courage to deny Ferrero victory when he served for the match at 5-4 in the third set, coming to the net on the second of three break points and supplying a perfect volley to level at 5-5. Ancic even edged ahead 6-5, but Ferrero made no mistake in the next game to force a tiebreak. The Croat double-faulted on the first point of the tiebreak, and Ferrero built on that good start to win the breaker and seal the match 7-1.

It was clear to Ljubicic that he had to prevail against Moya or the tie would be as good as out of Croatia's hands on the first afternoon. He knew he had a 100 percent record against Moya and was fired up. "Mario had given Juan Carlos a real match, and I wanted to do the same against Carlos, even though I knew the odds were stacked against us," Ljubicic said.

After making a bright start, the Croat briefly lost his rhythm in the seventh game. At 15-40 down, he missed with a serve down the middle. He then went for another ace with his second serve, only to miss the target once again and give Moya the first break of the match.

Moya served for the set at 5-4, but the Mallorcan's nerve deserted him as he sent a drive volley into the net when leading 30-0. Ljubicic capitalized on that error to break back and force a tiebreak. The Croat took a 6-5 lead in the shootout, and Moya gave him the set as he put a forehand approach wide.

The second game of the second set was to prove the turning point of the match. "I remember I saved four break points playing some really amazing shots, but Carlos was coming up with shots that I didn't expect from him and started to play really, really well," Ljubicic said. A double-fault on break point number five was to prove his undoing, for it acted as a shot of adrenaline into Moya's veins. He raced to a 5-1 lead, and double-faults on his first two set points were but minor irritants.

Moya edged clear in the third set at 4-3 and saved five break points in the next game to move 5-3 ahead. Ljubicic kept up the pressure by holding his next service game and looked ready to break back as he backed Moya into a corner at 0-40. Moya once again showed great guts to force deuce, and he saved a fourth break point before taking the set with a booming service winner.

Only one point went against serve in the opening six games of the fourth set as the standard of tennis rose and a state of nervous tension enveloped the crowd. Ljubicic was once again first to blink, putting a limp backhand into the net to give Moya break point in the seventh game and then sending an attempted forehand winner wildly long.

That was all the advantage Moya needed and, roaring on, he completed his 6-7(5), 6-1, 6-4, 6-4 victory by slamming down an ace on his first match point.

There were not many teams in the world that could overlook players of the quality of Costa and Alex Corretja in singles. Together they represented a formidable unit. And Ljubicic knew he had to take the strain in partnership with the inexperienced Lovro Zovko. It was no surprise that the Spaniards zoned in on the twenty-two-year-old from Zagreb. An overhit Zovko volley gave Spain a 3-1 lead, and when he was down three break points in his next service game, Zovko stumbled. Corretja's majestic forehand winner gave Spain the first set in thirty-four minutes.

Zovko held for the first time in the second set but, inevitably, Spain's concentration on him had its effect. For all of Ljubicic's urgings, he could not draw the nerves from the younger man's body. At 3-2, Costa set up a double break point opportunity with a forehand that evaded both Croatians as it sailed down the middle. Although the French Open champion slid a backhand return wide on the first break point, his aim was better on the second, as he evaded Zovko with a forehand into the tramlines.

The Croatians actually forced break points themselves in the next game, but Corretja managed to dig himself out of trouble with two deep first serves. From that moment on, the Spaniards were hardly troubled, lobbing, slicing, and volleying their way to a superb victory. When they led 2-0 in the third set, Ljubicic betrayed his frustrations, smashing a forehand toward Corretja that the Spaniard did well to avoid. Ljubicic later apologized but that apology could not change the outcome. For Croatia, the deed was done.

For all their efforts, the Croatians could make no progress against the Spanish serve. It fell to Corretja to settle the victory and he did so with a flourish of four unreturnable serves. The Spaniards had triumphed 6-2, 6-3, 6-4, and there was simply nothing left to say. ●

Pictured opposite:

Ivan Ljubicic (CRO)

QUARTERFINALS

spain v croatia

QUARTERFINALS
france v switzerland

52

QUARTERFINALS

france v switzerland

FRANCE v SWITZERLAND

THE CHOICE OF THE Zenith Stadium suggested high times and happy days for French tennis. Instead, they were to crumble to the phenomenon that is Roger Federer. The French had reached three of the past four finals, but it is hard to maintain that record year after year and especially when you are faced with a marvel like Federer. In the manner becoming so marked of the man, it was Federer who anchored a three-day magnum opus beyond the call of national duty.

The annals of this greatest championship are filled with deeds of heroism as well as tales of those who have stumbled under the pressure. Federer sits firmly in the first category and had already become steeped in the lore of the Davis Cup, a competition that lent him a new, unseen force.

In the face of French captain Guy Forget's amazement at this result, it was possible to hear echoes of the then newly installed U.S. leader Patrick McEnroe a couple of years earlier when Federer single-handedly dismantled his side in Basel. "We have seen a very rare talent indeed" was the McEnroe appraisal.

Such is the modesty of the man, that Federer himself is not quite sure how he does it. But there are forces working in him that render him a superhuman opponent in this most daunting of arenas. This tie was one that demanded everything Federer and his Swiss mates had at their disposal, and a lot more besides, and they rose to the occasion. Even the French were effusive in their praise. Philippe Bouin of the newspaper L'Equipe, who has watched almost as many ties as BNP Paribas has customers, said he could not recall a more remarkable individual performance.

Federer had needed to be at his best because, despite a decent performance, George Bastl was unable to defeat Sebastien Grosjean in an opening rubber full, eventually, of glorious French shot-making.

Grosjean began nervously, opening with two double-faults, but held serve thanks to a winning forehand, an ace, and a crisp volley. Sensing his early hesitancy, Bastl broke him in the third game, which, in retrospect, was the worst thing he could have done. Grosjean's dander was up and, though there was little hint that one hundred and sixty-three places separated the pair in the rankings, the Frenchman raced into a two-set lead.

Bastl's level clearly rose in the third set in concert with the intensity of the match. His first service percentage also rose and he began to volley behind it. The Swiss deservedly took a set, but Grosjean was driven on by the fear that Federer waited in the wings. Grosjean had to win the match and so he did, taking the fourth set in thirty-three minutes to triumph 6–3, 6–4, 3–6, 6–3.

"It's always important to win on Friday, when the number one is playing the number two. It was important for me to play a solid game, and that's what I did," Grosjean, a satisfied man, said later.

The onus was on Escude, who had been known to thrive in these positions before. His singles record was as good as

Pictured opposite:
Roger Federer (SUI)

Pictured left to right:
Nicolas Escude (FRA);
Sebastien Grosjean (FRA)

QUARTERFINALS
france v switzerland

anyone's but, in Federer, he faced an entirely different set of problems. Federer thrives on someone coming at him, rather than having to force the pace himself. After he had drawn first blood in the opening set, the Swiss number one settled into a rhythm that Escude found impossible to break up.

For Escude, it was like running into a brick wall. Federer improved his record to twenty-three uninterrupted sets of dominance in the Davis Cup with his 6–4, 7–5, 6–2 success, and the tie was level at one-all. "I don't think it was about him (Escude) playing good or bad, but more about me playing very well. I put pressure on him. I served better, and I believe I was the better player," he said.

"In the last few ties, with Rosset as captain, we've had a wonderful team spirit. All I can do is focus match after match and hope to win. And if it can be in straight sets then it's better, because it saves me energy since I'm playing singles, doubles, and singles again. But it is not something that daunts me."

As his performances over the following two days would amply testify. It mattered little that Forget took advantage of the rules allowing a doubles change, selecting Escude in place of Michael Llodra to partner Fabrice Santoro, but it did seem a strange choice. Llodra and Santoro had won the Australian Open title brilliantly in January, while a left-right combination was always felt to be ideal.

Switzerland had something better, a rapport between Rosset and Federer that could have profited the country more had it not been for too many years of wrangling behind the scenes. Rosset had the power in the serve, while Federer was grace and control under fire. His delicate drop volley on the first break point of the match set the trend. Even Santoro, that beguiling mixture of spin and speed, could not match it.

Though the French recovered to take the second set, the Swiss pair was tactically the sounder and less prone to rash shots. Even Santoro was not able to unwrap his talents to their full, which posed a real problem for the French. By the time Switzerland took a two-sets-to-one lead, the only player not to have lost his serve was Federer. Although he did drop serve to trail 2–0 at the start of the fourth, it was not to be a damaging setback, as Santoro was immediately broken back.

The next nine games went with serve, and the set went into a nerve-tingling tiebreak. There was a breathless hush in the auditorium, with spectators wondering who might snap first. Cruelly, it was to be Escude, whose second serve at 4–4 was pounced upon by Federer, who went on to serve out a 6–4, 3–6, 6–3, 7–6(4) victory.

The captain could hardly believe it. "I didn't really have an option but to play myself, and I've been in enough big doubles matches to know what to do," Rosset said. "I did not take many risks on my first serve, and by keeping my first serve percentage high, I managed to prevent them from attacking my second serve," he said.

"Roger is a great doubles player, he helped me tough it out psychologically. I didn't sleep, I didn't eat last night because I was so nervous to get on to the court, but this is a wonderful win for the Swiss team."

The final day was a blur of brilliance from the man in the bandanna. Federer won his third match in as many days to put Switzerland in the semifinals for only the second time since the formation of the World Group in 1981. Santoro managed to win a trifling three games from the Swiss superstar, who dominated the match from the outset, winning 6–1, 6–0, 6–2 in one hour and twenty-nine minutes.

Santoro had not wanted to be the whipping boy, but Grosjean had pulled a muscle in his left thigh on Friday and could not be risked. Within thirty minutes, the French knew what they were up against, as Federer rolled through the first set for the loss of one game. The second set was even briefer, and at one stage, trailing 0–4, Santoro was standing on the wrong side of the center service mark, so disoriented had he become. Even the French crowd did not know what to do, and as Forget failed to rouse his man, a hush descended upon the proceedings.

There was simply no stopping Federer. Overheads, drop shots, passing shots, everything he touched turned to gold. In no time the match was over, he was leaping into Rosset's arms, and Switzerland had confounded the odds once more with a fifth successive win away from home.

Another away trip beckoned in the semifinals, where the pressure would once again be on Federer for the tie against Australia. "It was a perfect weekend for us," said Switzerland's hero. "This tie had special meaning for us, because France beat us in the quarterfinals the last time we met. We'll travel to Australia with a lot of confidence." ●

Pictured opposite:
Marc Rosset and Roger Federer (SUI)

QUARTERFINALS

france v switzerland

55

QUARTERFINALS

argentina v russia

The River Plate football stadium loomed large next door, while eight lanes of traffic thundered along meters from the stand at one end.

If you took into account the railway lines in the middle of the highway—the train drivers liked to sound their horns as they passed—and the planes roaring into Jorge Newberry airport, apparently within touching distance of spectators in the upper rows, it was clear that immense concentration was needed.

Nalbandian was not distracted, breaking in the first game to set the tone for the match. After surviving a break point in his own first service game, Nalbandian took control of the set and raced into a 4–1 lead. Davydenko threatened occasionally, but was never consistent enough to worry his opponent. Even a short break for rain near the end of the second set did not interrupt Nalbandian's momentum.

By now the match was being played under leaden skies and persistent light rain, although Russian spirits did not need further dampening. Nalbandian was 3–0 up in the third set before the next heavier shower forced another break, and at 4–1 the heavens opened to stop play yet another time.

Upon the resumption—both players sporting fresh shirts embellished with national team identification—there was a hint of deeper resilience from Davydenko. Indeed, he benefited from some nervous play by his opponent, and it was with some relief that Nalbandian watched a final, desperate lob land over the baseline.

"It was not easy at all, but I felt I played pretty well today," Nalbandian said later. "I had a tactic of playing a lot of high balls which didn't suit him, and I think it worked. After the [rain] break, he was a different player. He played deeper, and he hit the ball better. But I wanted this win badly, and it is good for my team."

Gaston Gaudio certainly felt the breeze. He coasted onto court and coasted off it again, a 6–4, 6–0, 6–2 victory over Kafelnikov, leaving the Russian to muse that they had got themselves out of tight corners before but never, surely, one this testing. One break was all that was required for Gaudio to win the first set. Keeping the ball in play was enough for him to win the second, as Kafelnikov disintegrated before his disbelieving eyes.

At the completion of the set, the Argentine announcer started to play triumphant live music that did little to lighten the Russian spirit. Communication between captain and player—never abundant—had all but ceased. A disputed line call in the opening game of the third set, in Gaudio's favor, set a tone Kafelnikov could not alter. Gaudio enjoyed a run of twelve games, loosened his grip for a while, but then reapplied the screw, putting the home team ahead 2–0 at the end of the first day.

Kafelnikov was not as gloomy as might have been expected. "If I feel healthy, as I do, and I feel like I can win matches and tournaments, I will continue to play," he said. "And the crowd was excellent, too. I expected empty Coke cans thrown on the court at me, but they were pretty well-behaved."

Kafelnikov was back out there again the following day, in partnership with Youzhny for a doubles that would become, in all likelihood, a celebration for the hosts. The Russian flame flickered all too briefly, but Nalbandian and Arnold, who had suffered such grief in Moscow the previous September, were not to be denied the opportunity to exorcise that particular ghost.

The doubles settled into a pattern of frequent breaks of serve punctuated by the occasional hold, much more likely on clay than any other surface. Arnold, a touch brittle at the outset, was the man singled out by the Russian pair, and when they took the first set, there was a suggestion the tie might be extended. It was then that Nalbandian took a grip.

Stung by their first reverse of the tie, Argentina responded by upping their consistency and broke the Kafelnikov serve to lead 3–0 in the second, a lead they did not relinquish. The first five games of the third set were all breaks before the player of the tie, Nalbandian, held convincingly for 4–2 and the Argentines kept the advantage to win the set 6–4.

Breaks were again exchanged at the start of the fourth set, but again Nalbandian was the difference as the home reeled off three games in row to seal the match 3–6, 6–4, 6–3, 6–3 and a place for Argentina in the semifinals against Spain.

"In my heart I expected it," said a delighted Luza. "I knew it would be a tough match with lots of service breaks, but it was very well for us in the end."

As he spoke, the home crowd danced across the wooden boards, music blared from the loudspeakers, and champagne was being sprayed on anyone wearing blue-and-white stripes. The Russians trudged off almost unnoticed, champions no more. ●

Pictured opposite:
Lucas Arnold (ARG)

QUARTERFINALS

argentina v russia

QUARTERFINALS
roger federer

PROFILE

Name ROGER FEDERER

Born AUGUST 8, 1981, IN BASEL, SWITZERLAND

Turned Professional 1998

Davis Cup Records SINGLES 15-6 DOUBLES 6-3

FROM THE VERY START of Roger Federer's career as an outstanding, if occasionally rebellious, junior, they said that one day he would be the best of the lot. This year, he surely confirmed all that had been said of him—and how. It has been an enormous burden for him to have to carry on his slender shoulders, but his triumph at Wimbledon in July cast the Swiss in the role of leader of the young generation.

Those who have been preparing him for greatness since his early teens cannot be faulted for their vision: there is something special about the way he plays, the way he deports himself, the way he speaks, and his linguistic talents.

"It's tough when everybody is expecting so much from me," he says. "When they are saying 'Oh, we knew he would do well,' and then if I don't, they will say it is my fault because I had everything. I am in a bit of a no-win situation. Would anyone like to be starting out and everyone is saying that they are going to be number one for sure? I have been getting introduced all the time at home as the future number one, it can take its toll."

Federer is doing his utmost to live up to the expectations. It all started for him at the Wimbledon juniors in 1998, when he defeated Iraki Labadze of Georgia to lift the crown in singles (partnering Olivier Rochus of Belgium to the doubles title). He also reached the final of the US Open juniors, losing to David Nalbandian of Argentina.

At the outset of his senior career, though, Federer was not sure what he should do, how he should feel. It got to the point where he required the help of a psychologist to clear his mind of distractions and explain why he had the fire one moment and lost it completely the next.

"I was looking for help," he said. "I could get away with a lot on the junior circuit but now I was on the tour proper and I kept getting p****d off with myself. I was told I had to relax a little bit, walk to the towel, count to five, all these little things that sound so stupid but they worked. Right now, three years later, I feel so much better. I have stopped getting so uptight and it is important now not to become too calm, because that can work the other way."

Federer is well aware of how easy he makes the game look. He knows he has a technique that most players would love to ape. He is as comfortable as it is possible to be with his role as Switzerland's great hope, a similar position to Tim Henman of Great Britain and Lleyton Hewitt in Australia.

He doesn't know how his opponents cope (which, in fairness, not many of them do). "I'll walk to the net and say to an opponent 'Oh, you worked so hard today,' and they will say 'I had no chance.' I read press conference scripts about how they felt matches went and it differs entirely from me so much of the time. That is strange."

Not if you watch enough of his matches. The culmination of the Wimbledon championships, when he defeated Andy Roddick in the semifinals in sensational style and held firm against Mark Philippoussis in the final, illustrated that. He can only go on from strength to strength. ●

QUARTERFINALS

roger federer

61

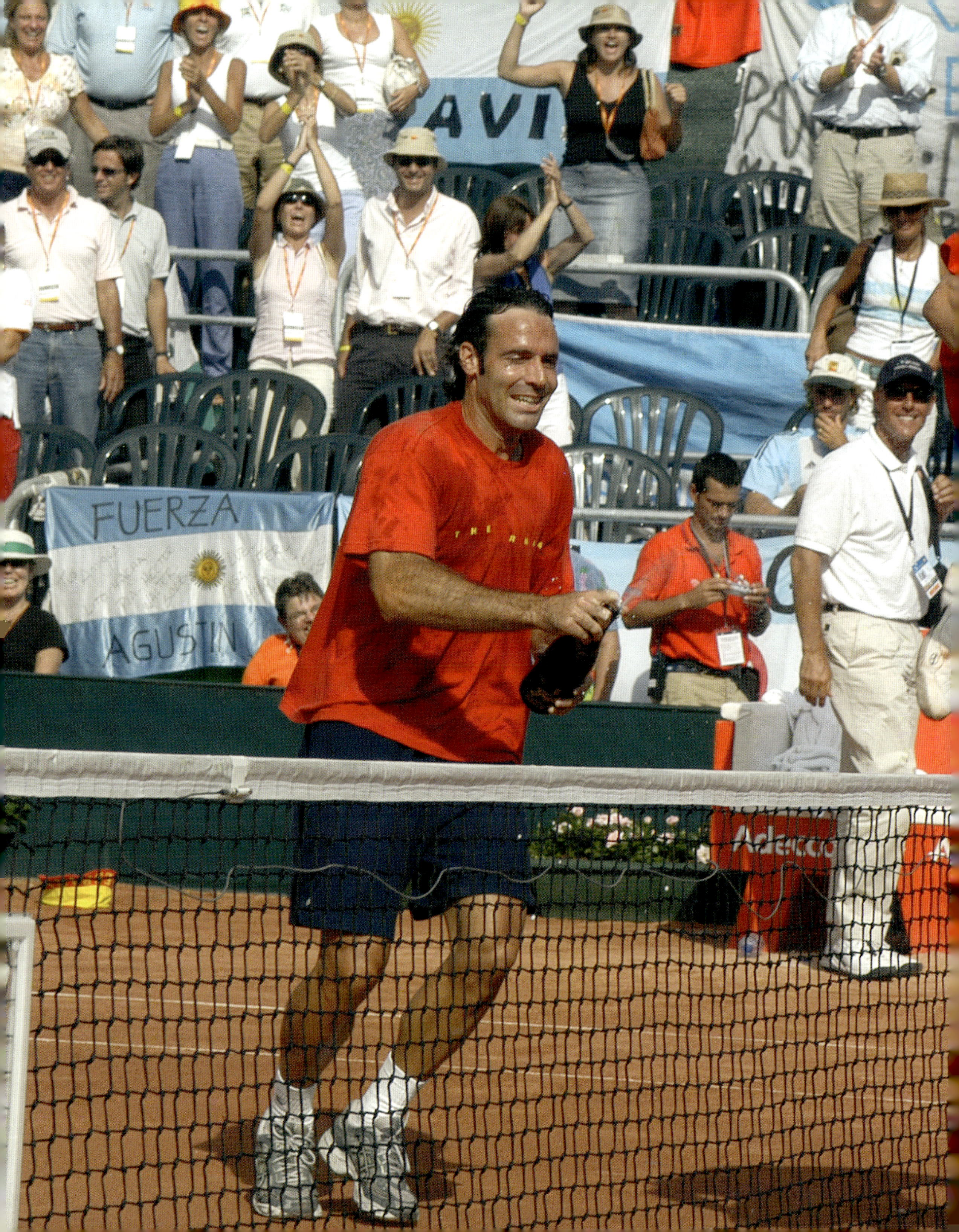
FUERZA
AGUSTIN

semifinals

Australia d. Switzerland 3–2   MELBOURNE, AUSTRALIA—OUTDOOR HARD

Spain d. Argentina 3–2   MALAGA, SPAIN—OUTDOOR CLAY

SEMIFINALS

australia v switzerland

64

SEMIFINALS

australia v switzerland

AUSTRALIA v SWITZERLAND

FROM WHICHEVER DIRECTION YOU approached it, Australia against Switzerland in this year's World Group semifinal meant just one thing: Lleyton Hewitt versus Roger Federer. There would be others involved, of course. One-man teams simply did not exist in the Davis Cup, so the prescribed theory went, but Hewitt versus Federer was every bit as riveting as Becker versus Edberg, McEnroe versus Noah, or, dashing back further in time, Hoad versus Seixas.

They were, for want of a more distinct qualification, the past two winners of the Wimbledon championship; the number one player in the world for 2002 against the player who could succeed him a year on; two athletes blessed with tremendous gifts, who played their tennis in two highly variant, yet successful ways. They were the fulcrum of their nations' tennis at the outset of the twenty-first century.

It was always going to come down to the meeting of the two in the opening reverse singles on Sunday afternoon in Melbourne. The contest would see either one of the nations confirm its place in the semifinals, or determine that there would have to be a fifth match to separate them. There had been just enough signs in the way Hewitt lost his quarterfinal in the US Open to Juan Carlos Ferrero for Australia to believe in him again. Hewitt's previous few months on the circuit had been nothing like they were stacked up to be. Amateur psychologists everywhere were trying to unravel the complexities of why he should have started to struggle.

All we needed was a sign that he was the old Hewitt again, the tenacious bundle of fire and energy that had steamrollered his way through the sport to such a profound effect in 2002, winning Wimbledon and the Tennis Masters Cup and ending a second successive year ranked the world's number one player.

Had he pushed his erstwhile coach Jason Stoltenberg to the brink too quickly? Was a court case against the ATP which threatened to drag on deep into the autumn occupying too much of his mind? Or was he supporting his girlfriend, Kim Clijsters, too much rather than spending sufficient time working on his own game? Hewitt dealt with all this probing and yet he had always stuck to one simple mantra: Davis Cup meant more to him than anything else in his tennis career. In Davis Cup, we would see the real Lleyton.

Switzerland's captain Marc Rosset, casting a glance to the cloudy Melbourne skies above, used a wintry metaphor of his own to explain the size of the visitors' task. If this year's quarterfinal defeat of France away from home was the equivalent of Mont Blanc, Europe's highest peak, Rosset said, then upsetting Australia in Australia would be Mount Everest. The Swiss needed three points from Federer and his doubles partner, and that was, veritably, a tall order.

The initial debate centered on whether this was going to be a tie played indoors or outdoors. The forecast for the three days in Victoria was pretty dire, but it was decided that only rain would close the retractable roof on Rod Laver

Pictured opposite:
Lleyton Hewitt (AUS)

Pictured left to right:
Michel Kratochvil (SUI);
Mark Philippoussis (AUS)
and Roger Federer (SUI)

SEMIFINALS

australia v switzerland

Arena, chilly nighttime temperatures notwithstanding. John Fitzgerald and Rosset met referee Jorge Dias for the traditional captains' meeting, clarifying the circumstances under which the roof could be shut. Australia's preference for an outdoor tie meant that the roof would be closed in the event of rain only, despite what Rosset had claimed would be a heightened injury risk if the temperatures dropped significantly below the opening day's forecast nineteen-degree maximum.

"There's no issue," said a slightly bemused Fitzgerald. "It's an open roof unless it rains. If there's imminent rain, [the referee] has the discretion to close it. If it starts to close and the radar is clear, we'll just reopen it, but if a ball is struck after the roof is closed, then the match will finish indoors, which is very similar to the Australian Open. We want it open. It's an outdoor event and we just want to play outdoors. They play footy (Australian Rules Football) here in sleet, don't they?"

Rosset claimed to be unperturbed. "I think we have a good team indoors or outdoors," he said. "There's not any preference for us. Roger won Wimbledon, which is an outdoor event, so he's a good player on any surface or in any weather. So I don't think there is an advantage for either country."

Of more concern for Rosset was whether to nominate himself for Saturday's doubles, for his preparation had been compromised by a back injury. Michel Kratochvil, the probable Swiss singles number two, had not been seen a great deal on the circuit after knee surgery in the spring.

Australia's selection was a good deal more defined, with Hewitt's touch improving and Mark Philippoussis moving more freely on serve, his recently stiffened neck appearing to loosen during his second day back on the practice court. In fact, his was such a fiery session with young hitting partner Todd Reid that the air turned almost as blue as Philippoussis's shirt.

"Mark hit the ball extremely hard today, even by his standards," Fitzgerald said on the eve of the tie, "and with our guys you can tell a couple of days beforehand that they start to get a few butterflies and they start to get a little bit more tense, and that's a good thing. It means they're ready."

Both of the opening day's matches were delivered from the threat of rain and gale-force winds by the closure of the retractable roof, which resulted in humid, still conditions. Hewitt, still heavy with a cold that set in several days earlier, had been told only forty-five minutes before the three o'clock start that the match would be played indoors. It would not have been Hewitt's choice, but by early in the third set—quite rightly, said Linda Pearce of the *Melbourne Age*—"he had found enough rhythm to have beaten Kratochvil in any conditions, almost anywhere."

Indeed, any fears that Hewitt's modest recent form would carry over to the Davis Cup court were unfounded. His serve did not fail him, even if Kratochvil's was not as shaky as he had anticipated. "My intensity right from the start was pretty high," Hewitt said, "just like it is in every Davis Cup match that I've played in the last few years," after improving his cup singles record to 21–5 with a 6–4, 6–4, 6–1 victory.

Kratochvil's effort was rather passive, almost feeble. Hewitt took less than two hours and landed a pleasing 66 percent of his first serves. Kratochvil did not have the weapons to hurt or at least he could not locate them and was bitterly disappointed with his effort, particularly on the return.

The second match was a remake of the Wimbledon final, won by Federer in straight sets against Philippoussis, who claimed he had learned a valuable lesson: if you let the man get on top early on, he will almost certainly finish the job. This was emphasized by the fact that Federer had

Pictured left to right:
Marc Rosset and Roger Federer (SUI); Australian captain John Fitzgerald and Mark Philippoussis

SEMIFINALS

australia v switzerland

67

won fifty-four of his previous fifty-seven matches in 2003 when he won the opening set. "And I'm not known for my fast starts, so I'll have to try to rectify that," the big man added. "I'll leave everything on the court."

Even that, as Philippoussis discovered, was not quite enough. Only for a fleeting moment, when the Australian led 5–3 in the third set, was there a hint he might make a real match of it, but Federer was coolness personified, winning in straight sets. The doubles would bear enormous significance and it more than lived up to its billing.

As he had done in the quarterfinal against Sweden in Malmo, Fitzgerald stuck to the tried and trusted pair of Todd Woodbridge and Wayne Arthurs. Rosset chose himself and Federer. It turned into a memorable occasion, one of the very finest ever witnessed.

"A fiesta of enthralling tennis," wrote long-time Aussie tennis scribe Craig Gabriel. It was made more so in that Woodbridge and Arthurs had to rally from two-sets-to-one down to win; and that Arthurs, the man who lost the fifth match in the final against France in this same stadium in 2001, appeared to be using the match as his own personal source of redemption.

"This is going to stay in my memory for a long, long time," he said afterward. "We were down the whole way and yet we came through. To be able to do that, on this court, in front of so many family and friends was a treat," said Arthurs, for whom the Rod Laver Arena became a friendly place again. "It's the best Wayne has ever played for Australia," said Fitzgerald in the wake of the 4–6, 7–6, 5–7, 6–4, 6–4 victory. "He and Todd were simply too wonderful for words."

And so, as we had anticipated, the Hewitt-Federer match would be very special. Hewitt to win and Australia won; Federer to win and Switzerland lived to fight a final match. It was the indomitable will against the extravagant talent, and rarely can Hewitt have called upon all of that will in such circumstances. He trailed by two sets and 5–3, and even his father, Glynn, who follows his son around the world, could not see a way back and that was admitting something.

By the time Federer served for the match after two hours, the man who had won thirty-one consecutive sets in Davis Cup had struck thirty-four winners to Hewitt's nine. Federer was within two points of victory, but a Hewitt

Pictured above:

Lleyton Hewitt (AUS)

SEMIFINALS

australia v switzerland

groundstroke landed right on the baseline, forcing an error that led to another, then another. "He gave me a couple of cheap points at 5–3 and I took advantage," Hewitt said.

When Hewitt took the third set on a tiebreak, Federer went off for an extended break, but his legs were heavy, his mind not where he wanted it to be.

Hewitt held for 6–5 in the fourth set but Federer flinched at 30–30 and served a double fault. An extraordinary save at the net on set point and Hewitt sniffed a wounded opponent. The final set was a one-man show of bravura and bravado, as Hewitt raced out a 5–7, 2–6, 7–6, 7–5, 6–1 winner, ending the match like an old gunslinger, firing imaginary bullets into a delirious crowd.

Both a beaming Fitzgerald and doubles stalwart Woodbridge said they consider Hewitt capable of regaining the number one ranking after his remarkable comeback. "If that was me, I'd be believing I was number one in the world, and why not?" said Fitzgerald, who also predicted an epic rivalry between Federer and Hewitt down the years. The Australian now led their head-to-head encounters 8-2. "They're going to have some battles over the years, those two, and, goodness, what a talent Roger is. What he can do with the ball, it's like a magic wand in his hand," the captain added.

Woodbridge said Hewitt could be encouraged by the far more dramatic slump—out of the top hundred and heading toward apparent oblivion—from which Andre Agassi was able to recover. Hewitt, twenty-two, had slipped from number one to number seven before the tie. "It's the first time in his career that he's had a lull. I mean, it had to happen; it was inevitable," Woodbridge said. "You can't keep up the standard that he did from the moment he won his first tournament there to the end of last year when he's been double world champion. There's never been a time when he's actually taken half-a-step backward—it's always just been better and better.

"Mentally he's just come off that extra high level of intensity and I think he actually needed to get a little bit of that stress off himself and being number one and the one being gunned at all the time. Every single player has had a lull: Agassi's had massive ones; (Pete) Sampras stayed number one for such a long time but, put him on clay, he always had them. This is really what's happened to Lleyton. I think it's just a process. There's no other player out there who has as strong a head as he does on the court."

Hewitt accepted the plaudits with modesty and grace. He knew he had been involved in one of the most riveting matches seen in Australia but it just went to remind people that he meant it when he said that the Davis Cup was the difference. "You can take your Wimbledons and your US Opens. This means more to me than anything," he said.

Federer, as is his wont, accepted defeat and his team's elimination with similar steadfastness. If only Switzerland could find a couple more players out of his mold, they would surely have a chance of taking one further step from reaching the final—which they had achieved once, in 1992—and winning the trophy itself. ●

Pictured opposite:
Roger Federer (SUI)

Pictured left to right:
Roger Federer and Mark Rosset (SUI); Wayne Arthurs and Todd Woodbridge (AUS)

SEMIFINALS

australia v switzerland

69

SEMIFINALS

spain v argentina

70

SEMIFINALS

spain v argentina

SPAIN
v ARGENTINA

IT WAS A LITTLE CHURLISH to describe Spain versus Argentina as the "other" semifinal but, what with the prospect of Lleyton Hewitt and Roger Federer locking horns to determine the match in Melbourne, the meeting in Malaga took on a slightly more prosaic hue.

The situation would have been a lot different had either David Nalbandian or Guillermo Coria been fit enough to take their places in the Argentina side, but they were victims, clearly, of the rigors of the tour, one that penalizes those who decide to take what may be described as a relatively easy life.

A team with them to face Spain in Malaga would have been ferocious indeed; one without them looked a trifle pale. Nalbandian had reached the semifinals of the US Open, and indeed he led Andy Roddick by two sets and appeared to have the match well in hand. The more the American fought back, the more trouble Nalbandian was getting from a strain in his abdominal muscles and a wrist weakened by so much tennis in such a short space of time.

Coria had said after his defeat to Andre Agassi in the quarterfinals that he was sure he would be fit, but he had been having regular treatment on a groin injury, and before he had walked out to play Agassi, had cut his right thumb on a contraption in his bag used to fiddle with the racket strings. To say he was careless would hardly do the situation justice.

It was with these situations in mind that the Argentine team captain Gustavo Luza had already begun to pencil in the names of Gaston Gaudio and Mariano Zabaleta as his singles picks. And so there were two ways of looking at the semifinal tie to be played at the Palacio de Deportes Jose Ma Martin Carpena, a makeshift twelve-thousand-seat arena on the western edge of Malaga.

The first and obvious way was to say that with Argentina's two best players missing through injury, Spain should have had an easy run to the final. But there were enough indicators to suggest it might not be quite so simple.

Gaudio was to open the tie against the new world number one, Juan Carlos Ferrero. They had played nine times, and Gaudio had won five of the contests. "We have known each other for a long time," the Argentine said, "and I know where he likes to hit the ball, so that means we have close matches."

Another factor in Argentina's favor was that the tag of world number one hadn't always been kind to its carriers in the Davis Cup, and with Ferrero back on clay after his impressive exploits on the North American hard courts, the time could have been good for Gaudio to strike.

Asked whether being number one would give a different feel to the match, Ferrero said no, but he did admit that readjusting from the hard courts was taking more time on the practice court than he had expected. "It's not easy to get back to the clay," he said, "but we're Spanish guys, we play well on clay, so we don't need so much time to get used to it again."

Pictured opposite:
Carlos Moya (ESP)

Pictured left to right:
Gaston Gaudio (ARG);
Juan Carlos Ferrero (ESP)

SEMIFINALS

spain v argentina

The visitors broke again to take the sixty-four-minute first set, but then the Spaniards roused themselves, breaking Calleri in the opening game of the second set, and then Arnold three times to open up a 2–0 lead in the third. At that point, with Argentina seemingly unable to convert any chances, Spain looked to be heading for the one point they needed to reach their second final in three years.

But suddenly Costa and Corretja were both broken to love, and when Calleri lashed at a Costa smash for a clean down-the-line winner, the forces seemed to shift to Argentina. A controversial overrule prevented the visitors from taking a fifth successive game and caused a delay of about five minutes while Luza vented his spleen at both umpire and referee, but Arnold and Calleri had taken enough of a grip on the match to hold their nerve and serve to take the third set.

In the fourth they were simply the better team. They broke Corretja twice as the two Spanish dads looked increasingly demoralized. Arnold said it was one of the best wins of his career. "It's a great victory, I'm very happy, it was similar to the semifinals last year in Moscow when we were 2–0 down and David Nalbandian and I won the doubles 19–17 in the fifth set. Maybe that one was more emotional, but this was very nice too."

Luza was refusing to commit himself on his second day singles picks, saying he would await the outcome of Zabaleta's practice session that evening, but the Argentine players clearly believed Calleri would open the final day after pushing Ferrero hard in a straight sets defeat in the Spaniard's home city of Valencia earlier this year. They were right.

And those on the sidelines would bear witness to their compatriot playing the match of his life. As they had made their way back to the stadium on Sunday morning, the people of Malaga were radiant in their optimism. After all, Ferrero was the best player in the world, clay was his kingdom, and Spain required one win to confirm their place in a second final in four years.

They had not counted on Calleri. The twenty-seven-year-old had played some fine matches in his career and was having the finest year of his career, ranked now inside the world's top twenty. He had beaten Gustavo Kuerten, Marat Safin, and Sebastien Grosjean in his time, and was absolutely not a mug. He idolized Stefan Edberg for the classical elegance he brought to his game, and there were shreds of Edberg's single-handed style in Calleri's.

From the outset, there was a wary, almost supine manner to Ferrero's play. There was little of the flow we had reason to expect, and he was being outmaneuvered from the back of the court. Calleri was making the more aggressive moves. A look into Ferrero's eyes told you he could not quite believe what was happening to him. Once he lost the first two sets, the third disappeared almost without trace. "The greatest win of my life," Calleri heralded the 6–4, 7–5, 6–1 success that made the tie score 2–2.

And so it came down to Moya and Gaudio. Well, it came down to Moya. Gaudio clearly had not recovered from the drubbing he had received from Ferrero on the first day, and when he lost the first set to Moya 6–1, he had played three successive sets of Davis Cup singles and taken just one game.

The only time he threatened was when Moya led 5–4, 40–0, serving for the second set. Gaudio played two wonderful points to fight his way back to 40–30, but when Moya set his sights on a giant forehand to take the set, he was not to be denied. Thirty minutes later he had the match wrapped up and sank to his knees at the end. Joy and relief washed over him in equal proportion. ●

Pictured opposite:
The Spanish team raise their hero Carlos Moya.

Pictured left to right:
Agustin Calleri (ARG); Carlos Moya (ESP)

SEMIFINALS

spain v argentina

PROFILE

SEMIFINALS
carlos moya

Name CARLOS MOYA

Born AUGUST 27, 1976, IN PALMA DE MALLORCA, SPAIN

Turned Professional 1995

Davis Cup Records SINGLES 15–6 DOUBLES 0–0

HE HAS DONE A bit of acting, likes to scuba dive and play guitar, has launched a line of his own men's cologne—with the slogan "Life is the most exciting game"—and possesses probably the most talked-about tattoo in men's tennis.

Carlos Moya is also an islander, from Palma de Mallorca, which tends to promote a fierce streak of independence. He is not as close to the other Spanish players as they are to each other, which is thought to be because they are all from the mainland and he is a touch more reclusive, as befits a man from the Balearics. He has a splendid home in Geneva, Switzerland, as well, while the others would not think about living outside Spain.

It is often forgotten that he has been the world's number one player, a position he held in March 1999 when he reached the final of the Masters Series event in Indian Wells, at its previous home at Grand Champions. The moment he realized what he had done, he joined arms with his coach and fitness trainer and danced a little impromptu jig on the court. Two weeks later, he had been replaced at the summit and has not been back.

By the end of that year, he was down at number twenty-four, a fall hastened by a stress fracture of his lower back that caused him to retire during the second round of the US Open and from which he did not recover fully until the middle part of 2000. When he won the clay court title that year in Estoril, it was his first since winning Roland Garros in 1998, when he was believed to be setting out on the path to domination of the sport.

In 2002, he was beginning to look like the Carlos of old, when he reached the final of the Monte Carlo Open, and then won the final in Cincinnati, where he beat Lleyton Hewitt for the fourth time in their five meetings across the year. Add to those the titles in Sopot and Umag (which might take a bit of finding on the map) and it was not a surprise that Moya completed the year ranked inside the world's top five again.

When Nike, his clothing sponsor, was looking for a man to model their new sleeveless shirt this year and neither Andre Agassi nor Hewitt wanted to show that much flesh, it was Moya who stood up to be counted and, suddenly, a man who had been voted one of *People* magazine's fifty sexiest men a couple of years before, revealed a huge tattoo surrounding his upper arm that caused many heads to turn.

At the age of twenty-seven, Moya may be moving into the peak of his powers. There is no doubting his physical strength at 6'3" and 185 pounds or the motivation that drives him to want to return to the number one status once more. He possesses a serve that is up there with the best, a forehand that most players would give their eye teeth for, and a fluency of movement denied him when he was in such pain with his bad back. ●

SEMIFINALS

carlos moya

77

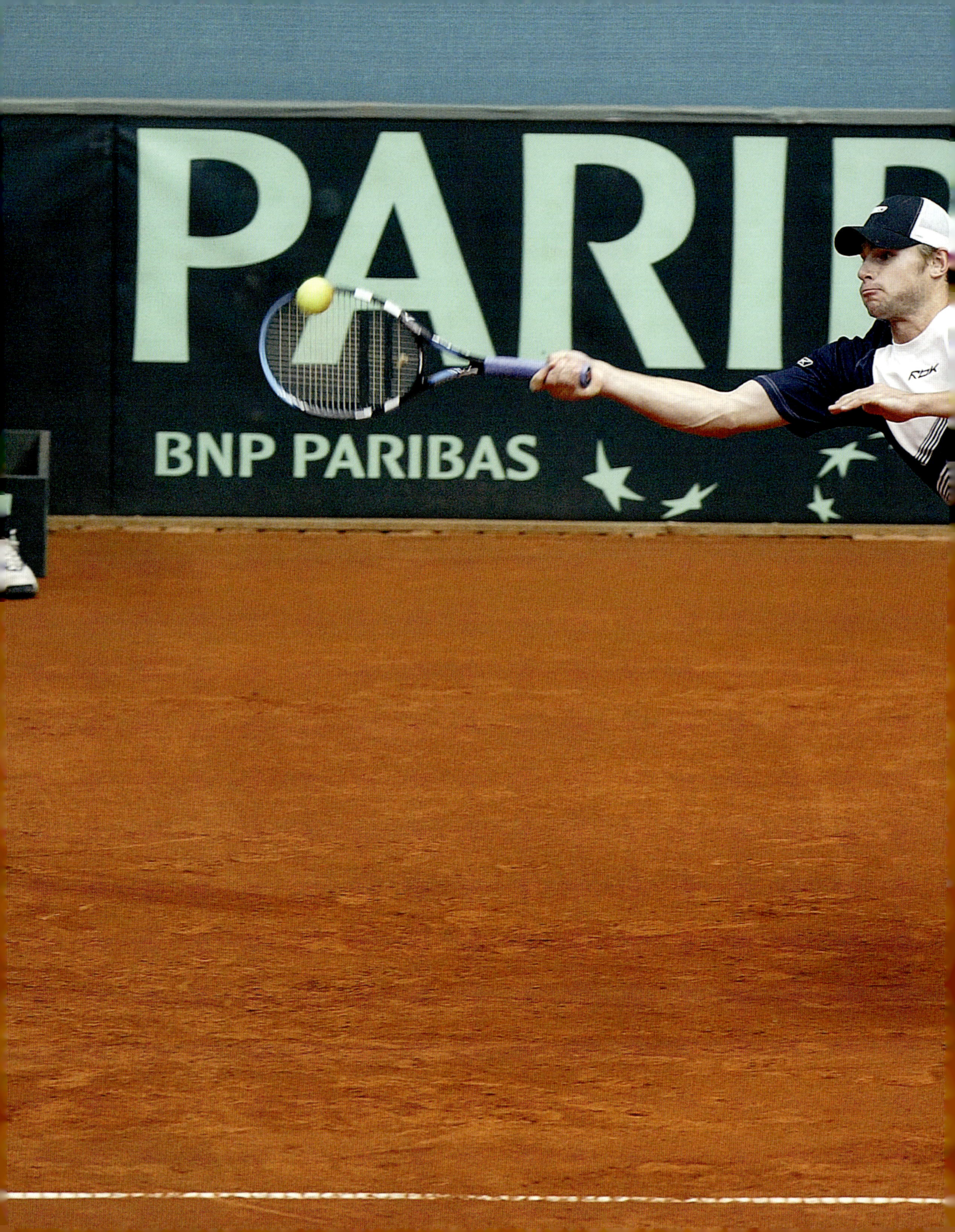
BNP PARIBAS

play-off round

Austria d. Belgium 3-2 PORTSCHACH, AUSTRIA—OUTDOOR CLAY
Canada d. Brazil 3-2 CALGARY, CANADA—INDOOR CARPET
Czech Republic d. Thailand 4-1 BANGKOK, THAILAND—INDOOR HARD
Belarus d. Germany 3-2 SUNDERN, GERMANY—OUTDOOR CLAY
Morocco d. Great Britain 3-2 CASABLANCA, MOROCCO—OUTDOOR CLAY
Netherlands d. India 5-0 ZWOLLE, NETHERLANDS—INDOOR CARPET
Romania d. Ecuador 3-2 QUITO, ECUADOR—OUTDOOR CLAY
USA d. Slovak Republic 3-2 BRATISLAVA, SLOVAK REPUBLIC—INDOOR CLAY

PLAY-OFF ROUND

morocco v great britain

80

MOROCCO v GREAT BRITAIN

PLAY-OFF ROUND

morocco v great britain

IT WAS THE EVENT in which the lights came on and lit up the skyline, and yet British tennis was plunged into comparative darkness. On the morning after the interruption the night before, Hicham Arazi was tossed jubilantly in the air by his teammates, while the crestfallen figure of Greg Rusedski was slumped in the courtside chair.

Rusedski, who had had such a wretched time with injuries, was asked to play three matches in three days. It proved to be the toughest of tough tasks. Indeed there were times during the second set of the decisive fifth rubber in Casablanca that Rusedski seemed on the verge of complete and utter exhaustion.

Contrast his emotional wreckage with that of Arazi. Who would have stuck out their neck and predicted, when the pairings were drawn, that it would be the Moroccan number two who would win both his singles matches to secure Karim Alami's side a place back in the World Group for only the third time?

The man in the spotlight had been Younes El Aynaoui, who found himself in the best form of his life. Years ago when his father turned up his nose at young Younes's desire to be a tennis professional, El Aynaoui paid his own way to the Nick Bollettieri academy in Florida, acted as a chauffeur for the better players, cleaned the courts, scrubbed the floors, and now, at age thirty-two, is one of the world's most celebrated players.

But El Aynaoui had warned the British contingent not to expect a clamorous full house at the Complex Sportif Al Amal. He said the Moroccan public had never really appreciated tennis and in the build-up, the lack of imaginative promotion was evident. The stadium's stands were barely a quarter full when Arazi and Tim Henman stepped out for the first rubber.

A small party of British supporters was there. "It's a long way to Casablanca," they chirruped. A few Moroccans jeered their jingoism. Henman came out into a blazing sun with a sore neck. He didn't feel good and found himself 4–0 down. Though he clawed his way back into the match, Henman could never quite get going.

"I was really nervous," he said after his 6–4, 6–4, 7–6 defeat, "I knew I was troubled by my neck but I felt once I got into the match the adrenalin would flow and I'd forget about it. The added tension just made matters worse."

All of which left Rusedski with the onerous challenge of trying to level matters against the rampant El Aynaoui. Early on the Moroccan was something of a soft touch, the British number two moving through the gears to take the first set. It needed that to get El Aynaoui's sap rising. He began pounding his returns, and the Rusedski game trembled.

El Aynaoui took sets two and three, but when Rusedski held from 0–40 down to lead 3–2 in the fourth, a new determination overcame him. At the end of the set, the Moroccan railed against everything and everyone, the balls, the court, the referee, and the prominence of Union Jacks in the stands. But he channelled his anger to terrific effect and won the final set 6–1.

Britain took the doubles—against Arazi and Mounir El Aarej—comprehensively and then Henman came up with one of the performances of his career, a four-set win over El Aynaoui of thrilling shots and, most relevantly, an appreciation of how to master the man on clay. Rusedski now had to come back out and beat Arazi, something he felt capable of doing.

It was not to be. The decision to turn on the floodlights near the end of the third set meant—under a captain's agreement—there would not be a fourth that same night. Arazi took that set on a tiebreak in which Rusedski had three set points. The next day, though Rusedski led 4–2 and had three more break points, Arazi prevailed, winning 5–7, 7–5, 7–6, 7–6. Morocco celebrated; Rusedski cussed. ●

Pictured top:
Hicham Arazi (MAR)

Pictured left to right:
Younes El Aynaoui (MAR);
Tim Henman (GBR)

PLAY-OFF ROUND

austria v belgium

AUSTRIA v BELGIUM

PLAY-OFF ROUND
austria v belgium

THERE ARE VERY FEW countries that can recover from the debilitating loss of their number one player just as they are about to contend a major tie in the Davis Cup, and even Belgium—in spite of being the biggest boom story in the sport—was no exception.

Xavier Malisse was in Portschach, preparing to take on the Austrians on a smart, pretty red clay court. He was nominated for the first day's singles but something kept on nagging in the small of his back (the lumbar vertebra to be precise) and rather than risk further damage, he made the wise decision to pull out. Austria sensed an exposed opponent and knew they had to make the first day count.

The stalwarts of their recent past were all in the stands: Thomas Muster, the former world number one who had lost only eight of the forty-four singles matches he played for his country in twenty-four ties; the terrier-like Horst Skoff, who often duelled with the best for the longest; and the lantern-jawed Alex Antonisch. It was an appropriate opportunity for the new order to shine.

Stefan Koubek had long been floating around the fringes of something special in the sport and he took no mercy on Christophe Rochus, who had gone to bed the previous night expecting a quiet Friday. What he got was a runaround, a thrillingly dominant Koubek losing only seven games in three sets in an hour and thirty-seven minutes, generating such power off the ground that poor Rochus was often left stranded.

Koubek said: "Today's rubber was one of the best Davis Cup matches I have played—possibly one of the best wins of my career. Things went exactly as I had hoped. He had no reply to my shots."

The second match appeared to be a case of déjà vu. The lefthanded Jurgen Melzer was taking similar liberties with Olivier Rochus, the younger of the two brothers. When he sped to a two-set lead, though Rochus had led 5–0 in the second, Austria had won the first five sets of the tie. Something had to give. Rochus began to claw his way back, cutting and slicing, getting beneath Melzer's skin so that he drew the match level. It was here that, rather than shrivel, Melzer drew fresh inspiration and raced through the fifth, 6–1.

Kristof Vleigen, the latest player from the Belgian production line that shows no sign of running short of components, partnered Olivier in the doubles. Here was a real contrast in physiques: the leggy Vliegen and the short, squat Rochus. However, the two players gelled beautifully, if a little unconventionally in their style, recovering from a set down against Julien Knowle and Alexander Peya to win 4–6, 6–1, 6–4, 6–2.

"They managed to cancel out all our good shots," Knowle lamented. "Rochus hardly seemed to make an error from the back of the court. In the end we weren't quite sure how to play them."

It was a tall order for Olivier Rochus to come back for a third day and keep Belgium in contention but my, how he tried. There is something splendidly old-fashioned about Rochus, and not just because his shorts come down to his knees. The power game means nothing to him; his passing shots are caressed, not bludgeoned; and he stuck brilliantly to Koubek in the first reverse singles for over four hours before the willpower of the Austrian wore him down.

Koubek had never realized such joy on a court, as the full-house crowd of 2,500 raised their arms to salute him at the end. Thanks to his 6–7, 6–2, 7–5, 4–6, 6–3 victory, the blond fuzzy-bearded Koubek, whose pale blue shirt was caked in sweat, had raised Austria back into the World Group. The old timers lapped it up. ●

Pictured top:
Stefan Koubek (AUT)

Pictured left to right:
Christophe Rochus (BEL);
Jurgen Melzer (AUT)

PLAY-OFF ROUND
ecuador v romania

84

PLAY-OFF ROUND
ecuador v romania

ECUADOR
v ROMANIA

AT THE QUITO TENIS Y GOLF CLUB, something rather remarkable happened. Ecuador and Romania became embroiled in a play-off tie that equaled a record that had stood since 1946. All five matches were extended to the complete five sets, the fifth of them held over until the fourth day as darkness fell across the Ecuadorian capital, the second of two twilight stoppages. The final, extraordinary conclusion, cemented Razvan Sabau's name in the championship's folklore.

Sabau first came to Davis Cup prominence in 1994 at a place about as far removed from Quito as it is possible to get—the Manchester suburb of Didsbury, England. In a Euro/African Zone relegation play-off, Sabau trailed Jeremy Bates of Britain by two sets and 5–1 but fought back to take the third set on a tiebreak and dropped four more games. Whenever debating the prospects of success for their team thereafter, the British media referred constantly to "The Didsbury Rule." Which meant: take nothing for granted.

Ecuador may now have to employ "The Quito Rule." Or maybe "The Lapentti Rule." Once more their nation's hopes rested on two brothers, Nicolas and Giovanni, while the Romanians could flavor their side with experience in Sabau, maturity in Victor Hanescu, and blooming youth in reigning ITF junior world doubles champions Florin Mergea and Horia Tecau.

The opening day was to set the exhilarating trend. The first four sets between Hanescu and Giovanni Lapentti were tiebreaks, Ecuador twice pegging the opposition back until Hanescu drove himself to victory. Nicolas was two sets up against Sabau—not a position the Romanian was unaccustomed to—but though Sabau recovered to bring the match all-square, the superior experience of Lapentti saw him to victory.

Quite how the brothers managed to come back and last four hours and fifteen minutes in the doubles remains a mystery. Unfortunately it was to no avail, as Mergea and Tecau took the one break point they were granted in a one-hour, fifty-minute fifth set, winning 7–6, 1–6, 6–3, 3–6, 13–11, before being hoisted onto the shoulders of captain Adrian Marcu.

Mergea, fresh from reaching the final of the US Open boys' championship, proved himself to be as mature off the court as on it, saying it had been "difficult" to maintain the pair's focus in the face of a raucous home support, but the finest Romanian prospects since Nastase and Tiriac were absolutely rock solid.

The drama had barely even begun. Nicolas Lapentti once again drew his country level after a riveting marathon in which three sets were decided by tiebreaks. In this beguiling atmosphere, with emotions almost impossible to control, Hanescu had match and therefore, tie-winning points in the fourth set tiebreak, but each time Lapentti managed to dig a little deeper. A tie that had been destined from the first shot to go into a deciding fifth match would be thus determined, but surely the light would not hold if it became another marathon?

It proved to be so, as referee Paulo Pereira called a halt with Sabau leading by two sets to one. There were five thousand supporters back in the stands on Monday, hoping to generate the atmosphere Giovanni might need to snaffle the two sets he required. He got one, but unfortunately so did Sabau, who broke in the twelfth game of the final set to clinch a 6–4, 3–6, 6–4, 5–7, 7–5 victory in four hours and two minutes.

Lapentti said: "I don't have excuses, but I think we had bad luck, because we had many chances to win and break opportunities. I think I played well; unfortunately I lost my three matches."

Romania gloried in their masterful triumph; not least Sabau who had never savored anything quite so rich. "We are not only a good team but good friends, too. There has always been a wonderful spirit in Romanian tennis," he said. "The doubles was crucial and Tecau and Mergea proved themselves real players." ●

Pictured top:
Razvan Sabau celebrates Romania's victory.

Pictured left to right:
Florin Mergea and Horia Tecau (ROM); Nicolas Lapentti (ECU)

PLAY-OFF ROUND

slovak republic v usa

86

PLAY-OFF ROUND
slovak republic v usa

SLOVAK REPUBLIC v USA

COULD THE MIGHTY UNITED STATES possibly be relegated from the World Group, with the hottest property in the sport amid their star-spangled ranks? It did not seem a question worth raising until the Andy Roddick steam train was spectacularly derailed on baptismal day at the newly christened National Tennis Center in Bratislava.

Roddick had become the spirit of the USA side, and there was neither light nor shade where his playing style was concerned. Which was not quite so true of the refurbished stadium itself. Faced with the prospect of variable shifts in light, captains Miloslav Mecir and Patrick McEnroe resolved to play half the matches under a retractable roof, half more in the glare of daylight.

"I see this as the start of our run to win the Davis Cup," Roddick said. "We have to get through this match first. It's obviously not where we want to be at this point. We'd love to be playing for the Cup this year, but it's not going to happen, so this is where we have to start."

Unfortunately for Roddick, Dominik Hrbaty was that start. The first match after a Grand Slam can often be a dangerous one, and Roddick, though he won the first set, was then outfoxed by the wily Hrbaty, who has been around the scene for enough years to know what to do and when. The USA had lost their previous four matches outside their own country. It did not bode well, the more so as McEnroe had boldly selected an improving player in Mardy Fish as his number two singles choice over the tried and trusted James Blake.

Fish did not expect to start against Slovak veteran Karol Kucera a match down. Then he was a set down. But it was here that the twenty-one-year-old from Minnesota chose to respond to his captain's faith in the most vivid fashion, striking his feared forehand with ever increasing ferocity and precision, sweeping Kucera out of the way to secure a 4–6, 7–5, 7–5, 6–1 victory to leave the match all square at the end of the first day.

Fish's timing could not have been better, for the identical twins Bob and Mike Bryan had just won the US Open doubles title and could not wait to impose themselves on this competition in their debuts. Hrbaty, in partnership with Karol Beck, was unable to raise his game to the level of his singles on the opening day, as the left-right combination of the Bryans swaggered to a straight-sets win.

If the focus had not been intense enough on him from the outset of the tie, Roddick could not possibly escape it now. He had not won a rubber on clay before, and the chance had been handed to him to make America a World Group nation again. Karol Beck was summoned from the substitute's bench to replace Kucera, who had complained of a sore right hamstring after his loss to Fish.

The American was swiftly out of the blocks, jumping to a 3–0 lead and punctuating the final game of the set with aces on the final two points. Roddick may have dropped his serve early in the second, but when Beck blew an easy overhead with a break point against him, it was more than enough incentive for Roddick to see through the match.

"I was trying to play hard, hard, hard," Roddick said after his tie-clinching 6–3, 6–4, 6–4 victory. "I'm just glad we got through. The team stepped up. The other day it was the Slovaks and the crowd. I wasn't going to let that affect my rhythm today. I was going to play my match, serve my service games the way I wanted to. We came here just trying to stay alive. That was our goal." And, at that, he unfurled a massive USA flag. Mission accomplished. ●

Pictured top:
Andy Roddick (USA)

Pictured left to right:
Dominik Hrbaty (SVK);
Bob and Mike Bryan (USA)

PLAY-OFF ROUND

germany v belarus

GERMANY v BELARUS

PLAY-OFF ROUND

germany v belarus

HARRY MARMION, THE FORMER president of the USTA and member of the Davis Cup committee, was the ITF's representative in Sundern. He had heard of Max Mirnyi, of course, had seen him a few times as far as he could remember, but nothing prepared him—or the Germans—for the Mirnyi who transcended this qualifier. Winning the opening match from two match points down was just half his brilliance.

The sight of the 6'4" Mirnyi being carried shoulder-high in front of them was one of those moments the crowd of 4,800 in this German outpost could not forget. That Mirnyi had beaten both of their singles players was depressing enough for a country that hankered over the glory days of Becker and Stich; that Germany would spend 2004 in the wilderness of the Euro/African Zone was very hard to swallow.

"Maybe the pressure was too high," Rainer Schuettler, the German number one said. "Tomorrow we start to work for the future," echoed Patrick Kuhnen, his distraught captain. In the room next door, Mirnyi and his compatriots were toasting the first time that Belarus—who only joined the Davis Cup league of nations in 1994—had reached the promised land of the World Group.

In his ten ties, Mirnyi had never played better, nor had he been more galvanized. He was two sets and 4–5 down to Tomas Behrend, who had beaten him earlier in the year in Stuttgart but was the surprise choice to play number two singles. Behrend then started to squander his opportunities, double-faulting at 0–40, at which point he felt a dryness in his throat.

At 6–4 in the tiebreak, Behrend once again was found wanting as Mirnyi crunched down a couple of unreturnable serves, and the increasingly anxious German played two sloppy forehands.

"I was a centimeter away from it, but that's all you need to be," Behrend said following his eventual 5–7, 2–6, 7–6, 6–2, 6–4 defeat. "Max was better in the last two sets and I could not convert my breakpoints."

He could not have known that it would take four hours and two minutes for some of the agony to dissipate as Schuettler defeated former Wimbledon semifinalist Vladimir Voltchkov, 6–3, 3–6, 6–7, 6–4, 6–4, to bring the tie level. "You are unbelievable, Sundern," Schuettler shouted to those spectators who had vociferously supported the German star throughout a brilliant match.

But he, and they, had reckoned without Mirnyi's sustained brilliance. Partnering Voltchkov in the doubles, the big man maintained his brilliant form to command a four-set victory over Schuettler and Nicolas Kiefer. The prize was within his grasp, but he had to take on the man who had reached the final of the Australian Open in January and was widely recognized as one of the fittest players on the circuit.

Still Mirnyi would not bend. But who would have thought he could win a match as significant as this one without ever having a break point against his serve, as enormous as it was? Not only did he send down a crunching twelve aces but rarely chose a bad moment to chip and charge, forcing Schuettler to search for the tiniest possible spaces to attempt to pass him. Mirnyi simply bestrode this tie like a colossus, spearheading Belarus's joyful progress into the World Group for the first time.

"Max played really good and that is why we have lost the match. Of course it's really disappointing for me. But we will attack again to come back to the World Group next year," explained Schuettler after the loss.

"The biggest day in my tennis life, for sure," Mirnyi said, reveling in his 6–3, 7–5, 6–3 victory. "Hopefully this will be the breakthrough for our nation. The rewards for this day are enormous. We have never enjoyed anything as much as this." ●

Pictured top:
Max Mirnyi is congratulated by the Belarus team.

Pictured left to right:
Vladimir Voltchkov (BLR);
Rainer Schuettler (GER)

PLAY-OFF ROUND
canada v brazil

90

PLAY-OFF ROUND
canada v brazil

CANADA v BRAZIL

THERE WAS NO MORE exotic prospect this seminal weekend. Frank Dancevic of Niagara Falls, Canada, had to play Flavio Saretta of Americana, Brazil, at The Corral at Stampede Park, Calgary, for a place in the World Group. Dancevic was in for the leg-weary Daniel Nestor, who had done his bit and more by defeating the former world number one Gustavo Kuerten on Friday. The tie, like so many others this sensational September, was poised at 2–2.

In terms of experience, only one winner could be considered. Saretta was a top fifty player, a flashy rock 'n roll–loving individual who often mixed brilliance with indulgence. Dancevic was a blip on the circuit screen, a teenager of Serbian extraction with brown, bushy hair and a diffident smile. And yet the Davis Cup had long had the reputation of turning the shiest boys into the most daring competitors.

Why the Canadian captain Grant Connell had a feeling in his gut that it would come down to Dancevic winning the fifth match only he could possibly explain. Did he know that Nestor would improbably defeat Kuerten, that Canada would win the doubles, and that Simon Larose, another reverse singles replacement, would lose to Kuerten, thus setting up the finale? He probably did.

Connell had known that Nestor, a doubles specialist of the highest order these days, was unlikely to survive the rigors of three matches in three days. He had played one of the finest singles of his life to defeat Kuerten 6–7, 7–6, 6–3, 6–7, 7–5 in three hours fifty-one minutes to haul Canada back into the tie deep into Friday evening, and had then anchored the doubles team to a success over Kuerten and Andre Sa.

And so in came Larose and Dancevic—a double switch. It fazed neither. Larose could not quite contend with Kuerten's desire to make up for the demoralization of his loss to Nestor, though it took a 12–10 tiebreak in the fourth to finally douse his flame.

Dancevic took charge from the get-go against a slightly nervous Saretta. "I went out there and played my game, I just ripped everything," was Dancevic's concise description. When Saretta looks back on the match he will rue the missed opportunities at 6–4 in the fourth set tiebreak—a skewed backhand after a cautious rally that gave the Canadian the confidence to put everything into his next, thunderous serve.

Dancevic dropped only one more point, winning the match 6–3, 7–5, 3–6, 7–6, after which he was mobbed on court by fans and media. A veritable stampede had come to Stampede Park. "Definitely my style of game was more suited to this (fast-paced) court. I hit the ball a little flatter," Dancevic said, "but these wins probably come once in a lifetime. To just be out here is a great thrill. To pull out a match like this—I can't explain it."

Josef Brabenec, a former captain and member of the Canadian Tennis Hall of Fame declared it "the best performance I've seen in Davis Cup by a Canadian in thirty years here." Which took some doing. Only two days earlier, Nestor had given a masterful display of serve-and-volley tennis against Kuerten and was magical with his touch around the net—as a preeminent doubles player should be.

Kuerten, who hit a Davis Cup record forty-seven aces and still lost, said he did not think he had done a single thing wrong in three days and yet Brazil was relegated. It was heartbreaking.

Regarding Dancevic's heroics, Nestor said, "he was cold. He hadn't played a match and he just came out really strong and took it to Saretta the whole time. It's unbelievable—if we hadn't won, people would have been saying 'why didn't you play?' I'm just so happy for him and for us and now we get to go to the World Group." The maple leaf had rarely stood so tall. ●

Pictured top:
Canadian hero Frank Dancevic celebrates with his teammates.

Pictured left to right:
Gustavo Kuerten (BRA);
Fernando Meligeni (BRA)

PLAY-OFF ROUND

netherlands v india

92

PLAY-OFF ROUND
netherlands v india

NETHERLANDS v INDIA

ONLY ONE OF THE ten ties played either in September's semifinal or play-off rounds was completed in two days. Elsewhere across the planet there were those for whom sleep did not come easy, but in Zwolle, the Netherlands, all was peace and tranquility.

That was, once Martin Verkerk had woken up and remembered that he was the finalist at Roland Garros in the spring and was now part of the rich Dutch tennis heritage. Verkerk had become the life and spirit of the French Open, barging his way to the final, where he eventually ran out of inspiration against Juan Carlos Ferrero. The chance was there for him now to establish a Davis Cup reputation.

His match, the opening singles against India's Rohan Bopanna, proved once again that strange forces can be at work in Davis Cup. With Verkerk standing fourteenth on the ATP Champions Race, and Bopanna, a distant two hundred and eighty-three, the match was widely expected to be a one-sided affair. However, twenty-three-year-old Bopanna extended a heroic fight. Never intimidated by the noisy home support and an opponent mixing fire and ice, Bopanna took a two-sets-to-one lead before succumbing to the tall Dutchman after a nerve-racking 12–10 final set.

Verkerk had a reasoning for his curate's egg of a performance: "Maybe I wanted to win too badly in front of my home crowd, because I love to play for my country and hadn't won a singles match before," he said. "But to be fair, this guy's really good."

Verkerk, whose tennis is as variable as his moods, not only had to withstand a young pretender playing the tennis of his life, but an orange-clad crowd of 8,000 at the Ijsselhallen expecting him to win every point. A loss always seemed unthinkable but the match hung in the balance until Bopanna's final forehand error put an end to four and a half hours of scintillating tennis.

It was not a surprise that, after such a prolonged wait in the locker rooms, Sjeng Schalken did not want to be kept hanging around on the court as well. And so he made light work of Prakash Amritraj, who already had the onerous task of having to try to live up to the reputation of his father, the irrepressible Vijay. The teenage Prakash only collected five games but did enough to impress Schalken that he has the natural talent of his father and requires a lot more of this kind of experience.

Verkerk clearly enjoyed the doubles experience a lot more than he had the singles. In partnership with John van Lottum, the big man excelled against Mahesh Bhupathi and Bopanna and was in a celebratory mood in the immediate aftermath of the 4–6, 7–5, 7–5, 6–4 victory that confirmed a place in the 2004 World Group.

India's experienced doubles player Bhupathi said: "We had never played together before, just like them, but they are used to playing high level tennis every week. Considering that, the score makes sense."

A bottle of champagne in one hand, the microphone in the other, Verkerk was asked if he would be participating in the final day singles. "We'll worry about that when I get up tomorrow," he said. "If I get up at all.

"As I said yesterday, winning such an epic match against (Bopanna) was breaking a mental barrier for me. It showed today because although I was tired, I played much better." Holland won the two remaining dead rubbers in straight sets, Schalken extolling the crowd for filling the stadium although it was sunbathing weather outside.

India will be back and so, thankfully, will their star player Leander Paes, recovering from a period spent in a Florida hospital for what was first diagnosed as a brain lesion but turned out to be a nasty virus. ●

Pictured top:
John Van Lottum and Martin Verkerk with Dutch captain Tjerk Bogtstra

Pictured left to right:
Sjeng Schalken (NED);
Rohan Bopanna (IND)

PLAY-OFF ROUND

thailand v czech republic

PLAY-OFF ROUND
thailand v czech republic

THAILAND
v CZECH REPUBLIC

THIS TIE WAS ALWAYS going to be all about Paradorn. Think of the expectations of any player leading his side at home, double it, and you get some idea of the demands on Paradorn Srichaphan in Thailand.

But ask Srichaphan who, among the world's leading players, you would least like to meet in such circumstances and the name Jiri Novak would not be far from his lips. Novak was among the most inscrutable players in the game's higher echelons. The Czech never gave way to his emotions, managing to stay in a cocoon of self-containment. You often wondered if you should check him for a pulse.

The frenzy of Bangkok would be perfect for Novak. The more hysteria around him, the less he seemed to bother about it. The Czechs, whose longtime captain Jan Kukal had been replaced at the helm by Cyril Suk, were below prime strength when injury ruled out Radek Stepanek, among the fastest improving players around. Bohdan Ulihrach, restored to the circuit after a controversial drugs ban against him had been overturned, was called in, though he had played precious little competitive tennis in the past year.

The first day followed predictable enough lines. The support for the home side was phenomenal; the Czechs were politely applauded; Novak defeated Danai Udomchoke in straights sets; and Srichaphan's 7-6, 6-2, 7-6 victory over Ulihrach illustrated both the exuberance of the Thai and the manner in which the Czech had recovered from his enforced exile from the game. Few had expected other than 1-1 by day's end.

The two sides departed from their original doubles nomination, with the Czechs deciding to play Tomas Berdych for his debut, rather than a recognized specialist in David Rikl. The home side believed the two players from the first day would be preferable to either Attapol Rithiwattanpong or Paradorn's elder brother, Narathorn Srichaphan. And there could be no charge of nepotism, as Srichaphan's father, Chanachai, was captain.

Rather surprisingly, it was from the greater experience that the errors flowed. Neither Paradorn nor Novak looked entirely at home, dropping their serves with impunity, and it was Berdych, rated very highly among his Czech contemporaries, who was the steadiest of the four as his team triumphed 6-3, 7-6, 6-4.

Eighteen-year-old Berdych admitted he was nervous to be thrown into such an important match with the tie evenly balanced after the first day but was happy with the way he responded to the challenge.

"It was very tough for me because it was my first match in Davis Cup and it was 1-1. It was a hard match, but I played my best tennis. It was perfect and I'm very happy," he said.

It was now down to the icon to keep Thailand alive—an onerous prospect. Srichaphan, perhaps not entirely unexpected, was subdued, in spite of the rowdy encouragement he received. He did lead 3-0, but even that was hardly of his doing, and once Novak got into his side, he negotiated everything Srichaphan could offer, even to the extent of holding his nerve in the face of what he saw was some particularly partisan line-calling.

Novak went on to complete a 6-4, 6-4, 6-4 victory and give the Czech Republic a winning 3-1 lead over the host nation.

"The pressure was on Paradorn because he knew I was playing pretty good tennis and he didn't really get the chance to attack me," Novak said. "He had the support of the crowd. I knew that would be the case, but it is not always easy when the people expect you to win every point. I am one of the happiest men in the world at the moment, because I won all nine sets of tennis this week and we are in the World Group again next year." ●

Pictured top:
Jiri Novak (CZE)

Pictured left to right:
Bohdan Ulihrach congratulates teammate Jiri Novak;
Paradorn Srichaphan (THA)

PLAY-OFF ROUND
max mirnyi

PROFILE

Name MAX MIRNYI

Born JULY 6, 1977, IN MINSK, BELARUS

Turned Professional 1996

Davis Cup Records SINGLES 16–9 DOUBLES 16–5

A DAY AFTER HE had led his country in typically barnstorming manner to its greatest Davis Cup triumph, Max Mirnyi's German website had not been removed from circulation, but there it was, proudly offering all sorts of information for a modest subscription.

Max is big everywhere, not least in the country that had cause to denounce him after his brilliant performance in the World Group Play-off that caused national rejoicing in Belarus. Remarkably, he has been on the international scene for a decade, earning his first ATP ranking as a sixteen-year-old. He is now firmly established among the top fifty in the world and has been ranked as high as number three in doubles.

Who would not want Mirnyi as a partner? Standing six-foot-five with a wingspan that seems twice that, he is just the kind of guy you'd like to have waiting at the net to cut off an opponent's return. Both Anna Kournikova and Serena Williams have been his mixed doubles partner and one wonders who crooked their finger at whom first.

For Mirnyi is not only blessed with enormous physical power, but his looks have earned him rave reviews as well, including IMG models who have signed him to market a whole range of accessories. The Monster from Minsk, the Beast from Belarus—you pay your dollar and you take your choice.

His full name is Maxim Nikolaevich Mirnyi, and he began playing tennis at the age of six under the watchful eye of his father, Nikolai, a one-time member of the Russian junior volleyball team. Nikolai has stayed at his son's side more or less since then, monitoring his progress, shaping his practice, and helping mold his son into one of the finest—and nicest—players on the circuit.

When he determined that prospects of a long-term pro tennis career were not too great if he stayed in Belarus, the then fifteen-year-old Mirnyi headed to Florida and the famed Nick Bollettieri academy, where he flourished, as so many others have. It was there that a mate, Alex Reichel, coined the nickname the Beast that has stuck with him ever since. It is not one that sits well with someone who is essentially a pleasing, mild person, but one you would not want to face across a court if his serve is in the groove.

At the US Open in September, during the interminable four days of rain that caused everyone to live on their nerves, Mirnyi spent every hour he could playing chess against the international master the USTA had brought in to help relieve the boredom of lounge-living. Not only talented but smart as well.

And at the Monte Carlo Open Players party in April, he stood up in front of an audience of his peers, with only a guitar for protection (he is a great fan of Pink Floyd, Jimi Hendrix, and the Doors), and sang a native Belarussian song in a voice full of emotion and passion. A little later, he was in the four-man group that spoofed the Village People's famous hit "YMCA", in the manner of IMTA, the International Men's Tennis Association. He has retained enormous popularity among his locker room peers, which is no mean feat in this day and age. ●

PLAY-OFF ROUND

max mirnyi

97

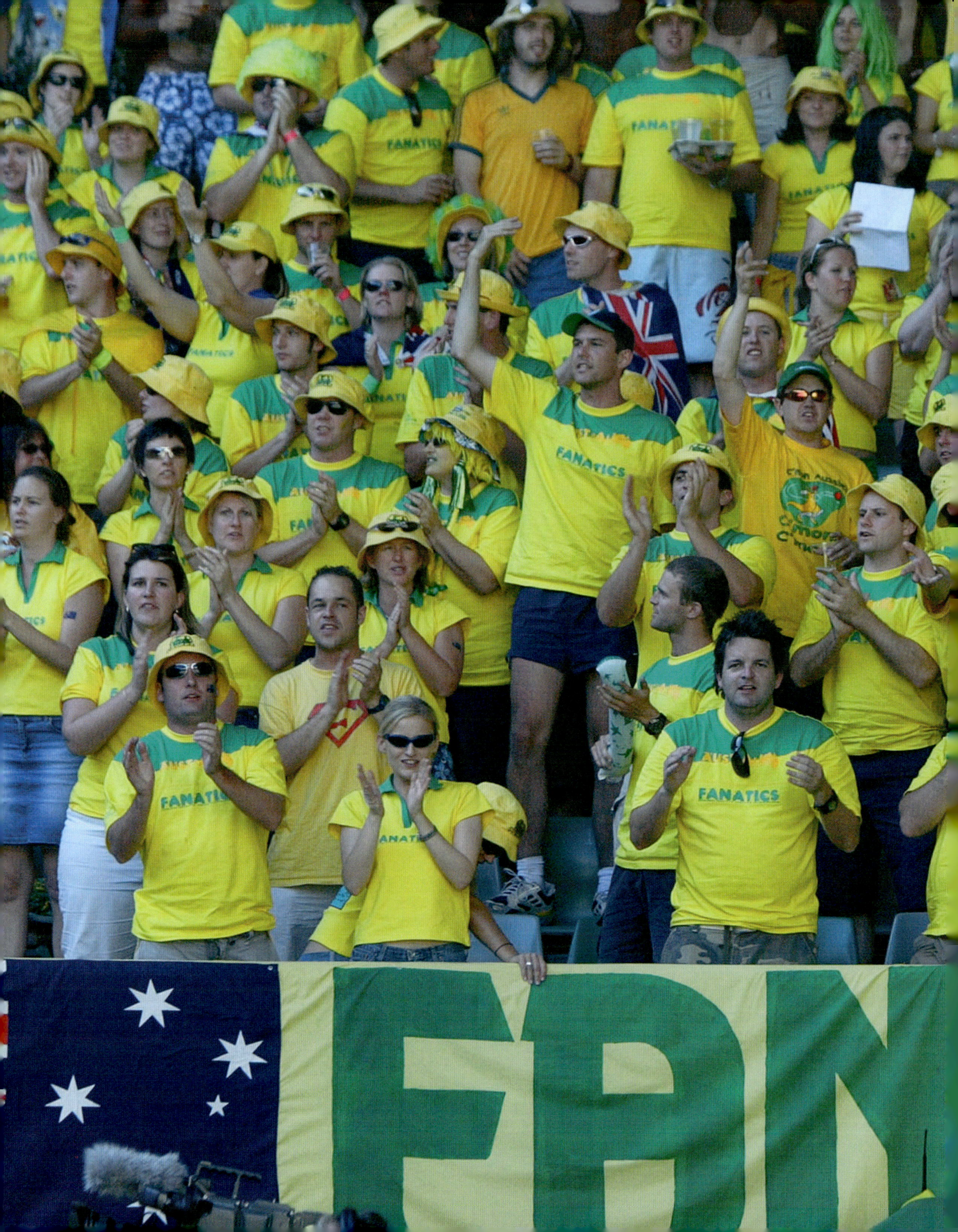
FANATICS

final round

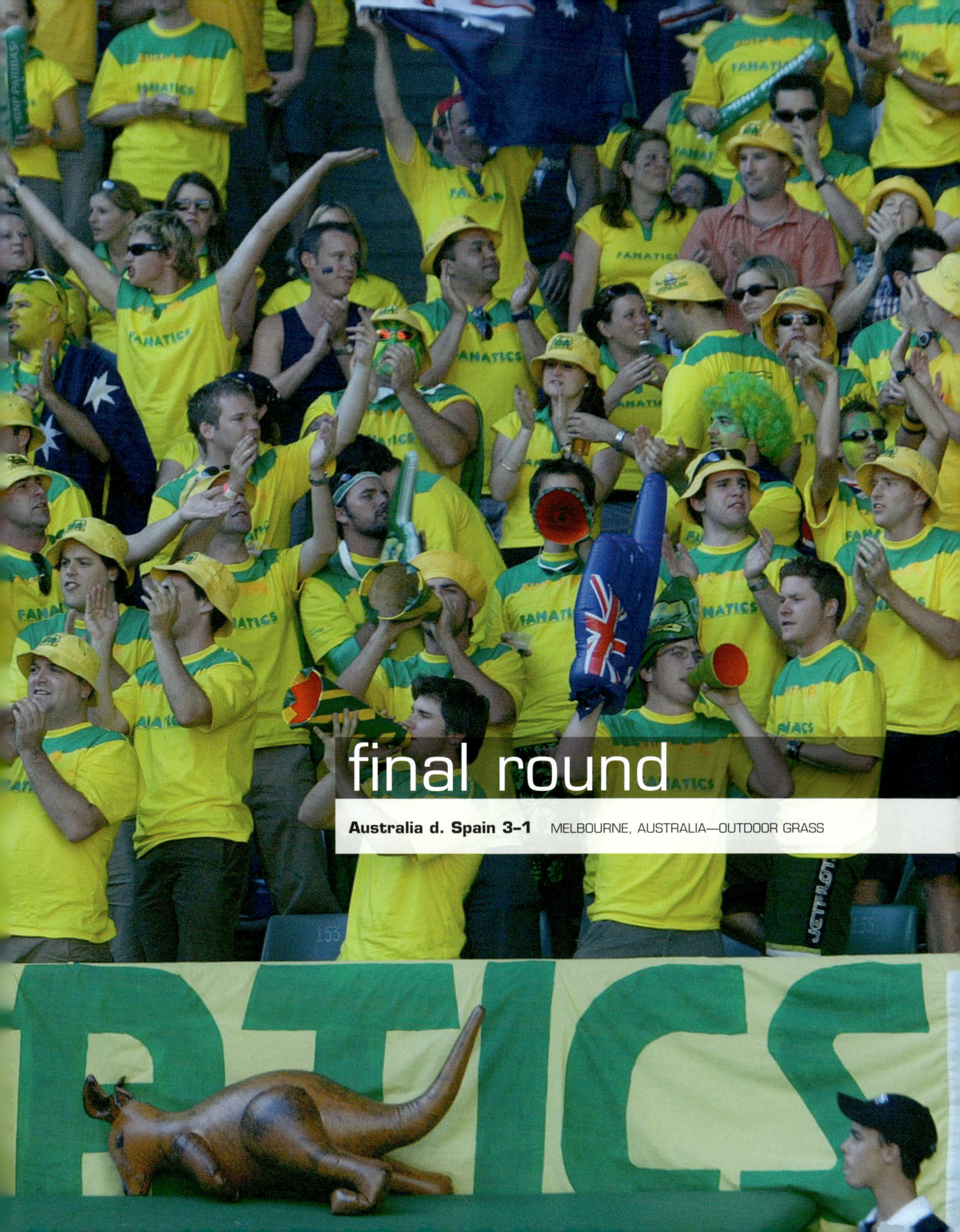

Australia d. Spain 3–1   MELBOURNE, AUSTRALIA—OUTDOOR GRASS

FINAL ROUND

australia v spain

FINAL ROUND

australia v spain

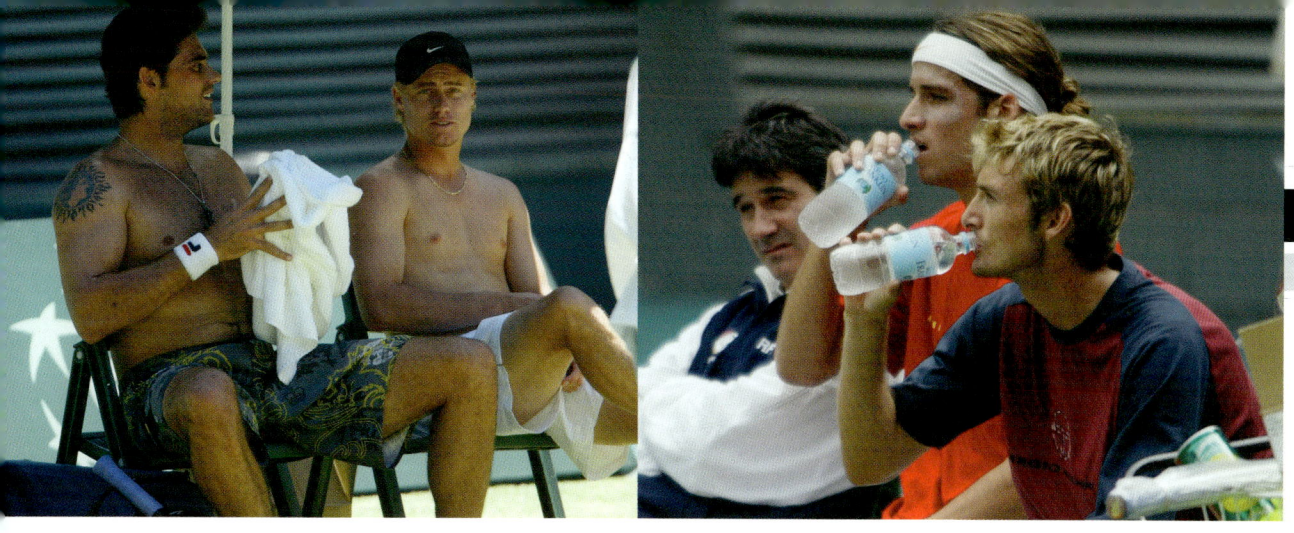

AUSTRALIA v SPAIN

IT WAS TWO WEEKS BEFORE what was to become the vindication of his life's work. Mark Philippoussis was sitting in the players' lounge at the Westside Tennis Club in Houston, Texas, not exactly being ignored, but hardly the center of attention. He was the ninth player in a field of eight, the substitute at the Tennis Masters Cup who had to turn up every day of the week and sit around just in case one of the prize eight had caught a cold or pulled a muscle during the night.

Though Houston is not far from the Gulf of Mexico, it has none of the luxuriant waves he relishes at his home near San Diego, so his surfboard had to lay redundant. He did little more than hang around, make small talk, and get in a couple of hits on the lush grass courts at the club, so it was a week of waiting and thinking. It was the easiest $50,000 he had earned in his life. But he was not to stay anonymous for long.

A few days' hence, Philippoussis would be in Australia, where he would not be able to move without someone wondering what significance it had. "I'm totally excited," he said, "and when I set my mind to something and start to get excited about it I'm a different person. I'll tell you now when I walk on the court for the first time there will be nothing in my mind except the tennis ball. I don't care who is on the other side, I will not even be putting a name to the face. It is just going to be me and that ball, point by point.

"I have a clear image of what I want to do. I don't look at it as though this sport owes me anything. If I owe anything it is only to myself. It is as simple as that. I feel fresh probably because this has been my first full year ever on the tour, one in which I haven't been injured with something. And my shoulders are still getting wider. My dad has told me that a male reaches his physical peak at twenty-nine, and I'm twenty-seven, though I feel about twenty-one."

Philippoussis started 2003 with a ranking of eighty-three and completed it at number nine, a rousing rise to a place where he knew he would be one day. However he had often wondered what effect it would have on him to have his game and personality undergo the forensic analysis that inevitably comes with such an achievement.

"Everyone matures differently, in different stages," he said. "I'm definitely a late maturer. I've always liked to have a lot of fun, still do, but I've learned that I need to live by some rules. I've really admired the way the Aussie guys like Pat Rafter and Lleyton Hewitt have carried themselves over the years. The job Lleyton's done for someone so young is incredible. Now I think I'm ready for that myself."

A fortnight later Philippoussis was front-page news across the nation to which his father had emigrated from Greece in the 1970s. "Green and Bold," one banner headline said; "Aussie King Kong scales new heights," roared another. The Davis Cup had been restored to Australian hands and, for the second time in four years, Philippoussis had won the match that settled the final. In Nice in 1999, on an indoor clay court, he subdued Cedric Pioline of France in the first

Pictured opposite:
Opposing captains John Fitzgerald and Jordi Arrese

Pictured left to right:
Mark Philippoussis and Lleyton Hewitt (AUS); Feliciano Lopez and Juan Carlos Ferrero (ESP)

FINAL ROUND

australia v spain

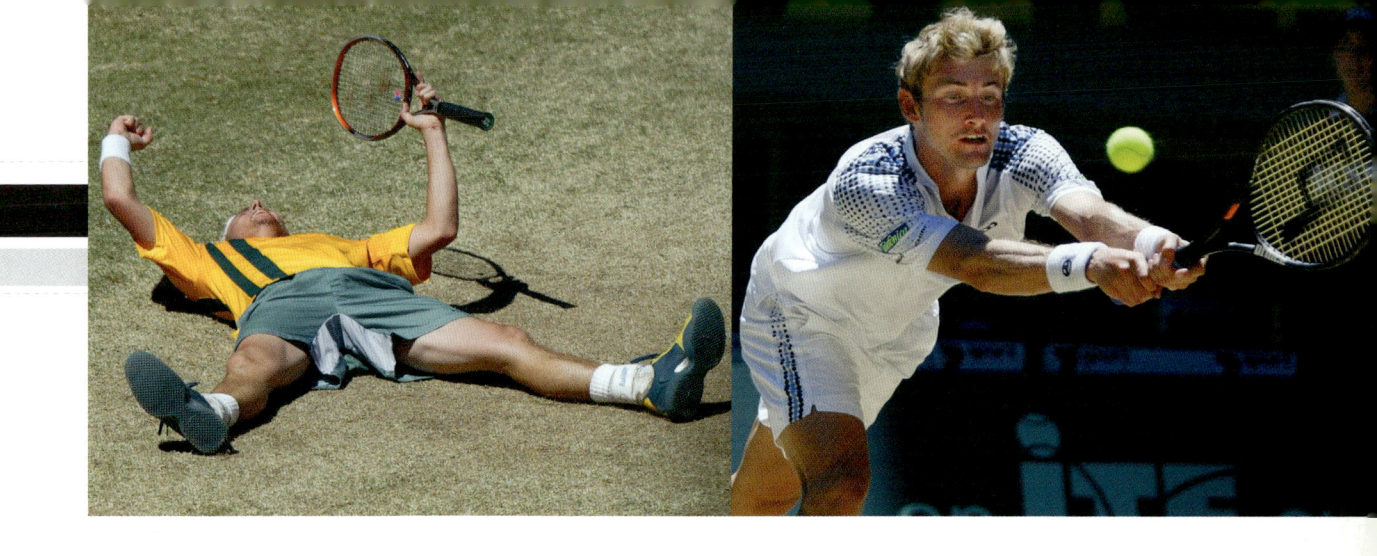

Pictured left to right:
Lleyton Hewitt (AUS);
Juan Carlos Ferrero (ESP)

Pictured opposite:
Lleyton Hewitt (AUS)

reverse singles and was carried shoulder high around the court.

But that was a long way from home. Of course, it was very special for him and his country, but Australia likes to see these events up close and personal, on their own patch. They had won the Cup twenty-seven times but not on their cherished home soil since 1986, when the present captain John Fitzgerald was a member of the side. To win it at Melbourne Park, the splendid venue for the Australian Open, in front of their own fanatical support was something worth living for.

Philippoussis knew it, and so did Wayne Arthurs, who had lost the decisive fifth rubber against France two years earlier when the Australians had first chosen to lay a portable grass court from upstate Victoria inside the Rod Laver Arena and the initiative cruelly backfired. Todd Woodbridge, appreciating that he was to break the record of twenty-eight Davis Cup ties he had held jointly with the great Adrian Quist, knew it as well. Lleyton Hewitt had been consumed by nothing else for months.

The Crystal Room is on the twenty-ninth floor of the Crown Casino, a tranquil idyll high above the ground where Melbournians pour their hard-earned dollars into a blinding array of slot machines that jingle and jangle but never seem to pay out quite enough. It was forty-eight hours before the Davis Cup Final to which Hewitt had dedicated his entire year and he was astonishingly relaxed.

Up there, you can lose yourself and feel as tall as the spires and skyscraping apartment complexes. Hewitt had not been seen on the tennis circuit since his semifinal victory over Roger Federer at Melbourne Park, which proved once more that he had a heart as big as anything he could see from this wonderful vantage point.

Actually, once he had been beaten in the fourth round of the Australian Open on Melbourne Park's proper Rebound Ace surface in January, there had only been one thing on Hewitt's mind, and it was not the successful defense of his Wimbledon title. The Davis Cup had become personal, which accounted for his mesmerizing performance in the crucial fourth match of the semifinal against Switzerland, coming from two sets and 5–3 down to Federer to win in five, settle the tie, and fly around the court doing an imitation of a demented gunslinger. "To be so far down against a man who is the real deal as far as tennis goes and come back has to be the most satisfying feeling I've ever had on a court," he said.

Goodness knows what would happen if it should have come down to Hewitt against Carlos Moya in the fifth rubber on Sunday and the little guy was to win—the perfect finale to an imperfect year. That is, if you base his 2003 record against those of 2001 and 2002, when he claimed his first two grand slam titles and ended both years as the world number one. He had won a single title this year, the Masters Series in Indian Wells and did no better than the quarterfinals of a grand slam. And he lost in the first round of Wimbledon to Ivo Karlovic of Croatia. Remember that? Hewitt could not forget.

A faltering summer period in America might have been rescued in the US Open, but he was beaten in the quarters by Juan Carlos Ferrero, who, by a quirk of fate, Hewitt would meet in the first match on the opening day of the final. "There were definite glimpses of my best form (in New York) but Juan Carlos beat me and then Agassi in the semis, two of the best performances of his life, especially on hard courts," Hewitt said. "I had been having trouble with a wart on the bottom of my foot for a couple of years and that seemed like the right time to do something about it."

Hewitt had not played competitively since his resurrection against Federer, knowing he was out of contention for the Masters Cup that he had lifted the previous two years and seeing no point in playing the European indoor season for the sake of air miles. Instead,

FINAL ROUND

australia v spain

103

FINAL ROUND

australia v spain

Pictured above:
Mark Philippoussis (AUS)

Pictured opposite:
Carlos Moya (ESP)

understood the match and that I had played a great match. It was an awesome feeling.

"There is no doubt in Spain that Corretja and Duarte headlined the whole situation and built it up into something [it shouldn't have been]. It made me even more hungry to win. There is no lingering animosity but it was difficult to take."

And so a fascinating stage was set. If the final needed any more spice dropped into its mix, it arrived as the two teams were being introduced to the first of three sell-out crowds. James Morrison, a famed jazz trumpeter from South Australia, was summoned to play the national anthem. As soon as the first note was played, people began to stir uneasily. There was not a hint of recognition on the faces of the Spanish team and, up in the VIP seats, two gentlemen later revealed to be the ambassador and the secretary of state for sport, had sprung to their feet, gesticulating wildly.

It transpired that Morrison had been mistakenly given the wrong tune to learn by heart and not just any old wrong tune, but an anti-royalist rebel hymn that was outlawed in the days of the Spanish Civil War. Another one seemed likely to break out at any time. Even Craig Willis, the peerless on-court announcer, was unable to completely soothe fraying tempers by pointing out the error and saying the right song would be played on Saturday. The Spanish team stood their ground, determined not to play until the error had been rectified.

Someone hastily found the right music that was relayed over the loudspeakers, but an air of indignation hung in the air for quite some time. Senor Gomez-Angulo spoke of full scale protests to Tennis Australia for this "intolerable behavior" and inquiries to be carried out. A formal letter of apology was rushed off by Geoff Pollard, the president of Tennis Australia, that was handed around to all of his guests and, as a penance, it was agreed that the proper Spanish anthem would be played before both the weekend sessions.

Thanks to Carlos Moya, the right notes were struck for Spain at the end of a day that began with such a discordant seizure. That the third day would matter for what happened on court as well as the music played across it was confirmed when Moya played as if he had been raised on grass, defeating Philippoussis 6–4, 6–4, 4–6, 7–6 to tie the match at 1–1.

The thought was that Philippoussis might have relaxed going into the second match, knowing Hewitt had played out of his skin to give Australia the lead by twice coming from a set down to defeat Ferrero. However, he was undone not so much by his own brittle play but by Moya's remarkable appreciation of the subtleties of the surface. This, remember, was a man who said on the eve of this final that he could not remember the last time he had played a match on grass.

FINAL ROUND

australia v spain

107

FINAL ROUND

australia v spain

108

FINAL ROUND

australia v spain

Moya should suffer loss of memory more often. His was a performance that would have had Manuel Santana, the 1966 Wimbledon champion, purring. We had waited more than an hour into the three hours and fifty minutes it took to separate Hewitt and Ferrero for one of them—Ferrero surprisingly—to play a volley. And he won the point with it. Moya could hardly contain himself, seizing every opportunity to take the net and make Philippoussis have to perform with steadiness from the baseline to pass him. That had never been the strongest feature of the Philippoussis game.

The big man was two sets down and Fitzgerald seemed to have all but given up on him, when something stirred deep inside. Maybe it was the rendition of Advance Australia Fair during a changeover—accompanied by an amateur trumpeter—that got him going. He followed a couple of blistering passing shots with leaps and bounds and gestures of defiance.

The concoction seemed to work, for he broke Moya for a second time in the third set to clinch it, when a wicked net cord spun a Spanish forehand into the sidelines. But it seemed that Philippoussis was hanging around waiting for something to happen rather than taking the match by its scruff. When he hauled himself from 0–40 down in the seventh game to stay ahead in the fourth set, the home crowd urged him to believe more in himself. Instead Moya regrouped and from 0–2 down played an impeccable, match-clinching tiebreak.

Tiebreaks were to be the high points of the opening day played in temperatures that touched thirty-three degrees Celsius. There can have been few better tiebreaks in the year than that played by Hewitt to turn his match against Ferrero on its head. At two-sets-to-one down to the Spanish number one, who had beaten him in the quarterfinals of the US Open, Hewitt knew that this sudden death was truly make-or-break. Lose it and maybe his country's entire chance of lifting the Cup would disappear.

After he won the second point, having lost his footing in the rally, Hewitt did not look back. He raced through it 7–0, broke Ferrero's first service game of the fifth to love, and would have led 3–0 had Ferrero not come up with two backhand volleys in consecutive shots to deny him a second break. But Hewitt remained utterly resolute, running off nine points in succession to break his opponent's spirit and set up the 3–6, 6–3, 3–6, 7–6, 6–2 victory that improved his Davis Cup singles win-loss record to an astonishing 21–5. "He's just a special kid," Fitzgerald said. "If he hasn't won the hearts of the nation now, he never will."

The neutrals love these ties to be tied at 1–1 at the end of the first day, guaranteeing that the Sunday will be pivotal. We had what we wanted. And it was time for the Australians to wallow in some Davis Cup nostalgia. Colin Long, the eldest surviving Davis Cup player to be granted a hero's welcome at Melbourne Park to open the Saturday proceedings, was number 32 on the list; Frank Sedgman, looking full of beans, was number 36; Rex Hartwig number 42; and Ken Rosewall, ever sprightly a half-century from his debut, number 43.

An explanation? Tennis Australia had followed cricket's initiative and introduced numbers to signify where players first took their place on the nation's roll of honor in an event they have long regarded with a protective affection. Woodbridge and Arthurs, with the numbers 83 and 90 stitched proudly onto their team tracksuits, were then to treat the tough-skinned legends to a doubles performance they would probably not have seen bettered in all their many years.

Pat Cash (number 74)—golden hair highlights, glinting left earring and all—had been inducted into Australia's Davis Cup Hall of Fame before proceedings began and it was doubtful if even he, a brilliant exponent of doubles, ever touched the levels of the two thirty-two-year-olds who played a brand of tennis in dazzling concert with the blue skies overhead.

Pictured opposite:
Todd Woodbridge and Wayne Arthurs (AUS)

Pictured left to right:
Feliciano Lopez and Alex Corretja (ESP); Todd Woodbridge and Wayne Arthurs (AUS)

FINAL ROUND
australia v spain

With their 6–3, 6–1, 6–3 destruction of Corretja and Lopez, the Aussie pair guaranteed their side would enter the final day needing one of Philippoussis and Hewitt to win their singles and guarantee that first home victory since Cash was living the high life in 1986. Woodbridge had amassed seventy-eight doubles titles in his career, eight of those at Wimbledon, and never, in all that time, did one remember him dancing such a delirious jig as he did at the climax to this crushing victory.

It had to have been the manner of his performance that caused him to react so much out of self-possessed character, for it was barely touched by error and was full of piercing returns, secure serving, dramatic interceptions, and best of all, a series of lobs, both defensive and aggressive, that tore the heart out of the Spanish resistance. Fitzgerald was moved to describe Woodbridge as a doubles maestro, a master of his craft. Corretja said that the Australian performance had come from "out of this planet."

Woodbridge and Arthurs only come together for the Davis Cup. Woodbridge plays his doubles these days with Sweden's Jonas Bjorkman and Arthurs with Paul Hanley. Goodness knows how good they might be if they actually struck up a long-term accord. "Oh go on Todd, please, please let me win one grand slam with you," Arthurs said, bouncing up and down in his chair as if a little kid wanting a parent to let them have their favorite comforter.

It was one of those very special days to be an Australian. The sight of their prime minister, John Howard, joining in a chorus of *Waltzing Matilda* with the "Fanatics," who took over their usual corner of the Rod Laver Arena, lent the occasion a special blend of humor and effervescence. They not only give their own side incredible support but rarely let the opposition rest easy for long. Corretja was their target, as the tune of Tom Jones's *Delilah* chorused "Why, why, why Corretja?"

The Australian supporters were unashamedly playing on the decision to select him, a choice that been perilously difficult for Arrese. Corretja had been miserably out of form in 2003, to the extent that he had played a challenger event in Bratislava a couple of weeks before the final to see if that might allow him a few wins to boost his malign confidence.

From the moment he was beaten in the first round of the Australian Open by the twenty-year-old lefthander who stood in his corner yesterday, Corretja had been on the slide. His singles record coming into Melbourne was fourteen wins and twenty-three losses and in doubles, he had won eight and lost twelve. Arrese had to decide whether to stick with Corretja, who said that he had been a fighter all his way and would be the same until the day he died, or bring in Albert Costa, a former grand slam singles winner but hardly a terrorizing influence on grass.

Arrese could have asked Costa to leap on Corretja's shoulders and it wouldn't have made much difference. A break of Corretja's first service game to love, as the Australian pair nailed four at-his-toes returns, set a trend of home-brewed excellence the Spaniards could not quell. When Lopez, who reached the fourth round of Wimbledon in 2002, lost his serve from 40–0 in the fifth game of the second set, the roll was in irresistible motion.

Corretja was not playing well enough himself to help his young partner through a match when no allowances were made for his immaturity. The Spaniards were taken apart, piece by aggravating piece, and nothing they tried worked. The end was mercifully quick, an hour and thirty-four minutes to put Corretja and Lopez in their place. Woodbridge said that only in a couple of his Wimbledon triumphs with the watching Mark Woodforde had he touched that standard of play.

"I didn't feel that great in our first warm-up today but then, in the actual warm-up for the match I had a racket that just felt fantastic, and just as Wayne went out to serve the first game I said 'Gee, it feels really good out here.' That

---

Pictured left to right:
Mark Philippoussis (AUS);
Juan Carlos Ferrero (ESP)

Pictured opposite:
Mark Philippoussis (AUS)

FINAL ROUND

australia v spain

111

FINAL ROUND

australia v spain

112

FINAL ROUND

australia v spain

feeling hasn't stopped since." Fitzgerald took up the theme: "I think these two, right now, are the best doubles team in the world," he said. "To have them play so well this year has been an inspiration for me. I want to thank them both publicly."

Reflecting on the joyous hugs given Woodbridge and Arthurs at the side of the court by Philippoussis and Hewitt, the captain added: "You can take a lot of positive feelings when a team plays to that level and gets a point on the board, but there are no celebrations in our locker room right now. They were all quiet and reserved in there. There is still a long way to go. There really is."

When Ferrero seized the third and fourth sets to level the fourth rubber at two sets all against Philippoussis, those words from Fitzgerald resonated through the corridors of the stadium. The famed Philippoussis serve had been broken twice to love at the end of the fourth set. He had won only two points from the previous four games and did not seem to have anything left in his oft-battered legs or memory bank.

The most extraordinary half an hour of his life later and he was being feted in a manner he can only have imagined in his weirdest dreams. Philippoussis had been accused of not treating the Cup with the respect it deserved, and there were those who felt he did not properly appreciate what all the fuss was about. When he fell back onto the grass, a last smash having burned a hole just where he wanted it to, he was up there with the Davis Cup Gods. There could be no doubting him ever again.

Philippoussis had defeated Ferrero, the Spanish number one and world number three, 7–5, 6–3, 1–6, 2–6, 6–0, the last set of which is bound to be the subject of dinner table reminiscences for as long as those there to see it want to talk it through. The twenty-seven-year-old's win gave his country an unassailable 3–1 lead and provoked scenes of rapture and rejoicing as he staggered into the arms of the teary-eyed Fitzgerald and was almost swept off his wobbly legs by Hewitt, who had finally emerged from the locker room at 5–0 in the fifth, suspecting there was no way his new best mate could lose from there.

They were joined in the delirious huddle by Woodbridge and Arthurs and how sweet this was for all of them, for each member of the team had won a match, glory finding equal favor. And yet Philippoussis, hoisted aloft in Nice those four years ago, seemed more equal than the rest. It may be the way he looks, with the intimidating frame, bronzed features, and thick sweep of black hair, a combination he has perhaps never used to quite the effect he should. He will properly point to cruel luck with injuries, a sequence that began on Centre Court at Wimbledon in 1999, when he crumpled trying to return a Pete Sampras serve.

He underwent two operations in 2000 and a third in 2001, when synthetic cartilage was fused into his left knee, requiring six months of rehabilitation, two months of which was spent in a wheelchair. "I was in so much pain. I needed to take so many painkillers I would probably sleep for fifteen hours a day," he said. "The doctors said I might never play again but I was determined what wouldn't happen. It just made me want this more."

Philippoussis has been a notoriously hard person to handle, coaches have come and gone, and this year he decided he would work exclusively with Nick, his father, who emigrated here from Greece in the mid-seventies. "If he hadn't pushed me, I'd probably be putting food on supermarket shelves now, so I'm pretty thankful for him," Philippoussis said. Seeing his dad—who has beaten leukemia—wiping tears of joy from his face in the tumultuous aftermath of the Australian victory yesterday did a son's heart good.

The match had not quite gone as a coach would plan. Philippoussis actually jogged out into the light of the stadium, whose roof had been drawn back after bolts of electricity that lit up the morning skyline had been swept to

Pictured opposite:
Lleyton Hewitt and
Mark Philippoussis (AUS)

Pictured left to right:
Australia celebrates its victory;
Australian Prime Minister
John Howard

FINAL ROUND

australia v spain

Pictured above:
ITF President Francesco Ricci Bitti presents the Davis Cup trophy to John Fitzgerald.

Pictured opposite:
Australia's winning Davis Cup team.

sea. He had to see off two break points in his first service game that lasted six minutes. The tension was palpable. The only break came in the set-clinching twelfth game, when Philippoussis reacted to a clinching forehand volley winner with a roar as deafening as any thunderclap.

One break was decisive for the Australian number one to win the second set but, as let downs go, his was a big one, losing serve for the first time in the second game of the third set that included seven deuces, four double-faults, and seven break points before he planted a backhand volley a yard long. Ferrero was now rolling in his passing shots, his eye was in, and by the time he had broken Philippoussis a further three times, the match was tied at two sets all and, in the stadium's bowels, Hewitt was well into his sprinting drills preparing for a fifth rubber against Carlos Moya.

It was then that having a chiropractor on the books came to their aid. Andrea Bisaz, who travels full time with Hewitt, laid on some heavy-handed twisting and bending of the Philippoussis right arm and rubbed warm cream into his chest muscles. The effect was astonishing. Ferrero, who had had all the momentum, was rocked back. "I just told Mark he had to play through the pain, put it out of his mind," Fitzgerald said. "I said he had to start off strongly, hold his first serve, start chipping and coming in quickly, put some pressure on him, and he might start missing a couple. And he did."

More than a couple, Ferrero started to miss everything. Philippoussis was playing on raw adrenaline, and it propelled him to a near faultless set. Ferrero saved one match point with a peerless backhand pass, but Philippoussis was all over him on the second and smashed away a pale, lifeless lob. "This is the Davis Cup and you leave your heart out there," Philippoussis said later. "That fifth set was just weird." Weird and simply wonderful. ●

FINAL ROUND

australia v spain

115

FINAL ROUND

mark philippoussis

PROFILE

Name	MARK PHILIPPOUSSIS
Born	NOVEMBER 7, 1976, IN MELBOURNE, AUSTRALIA
Turned Professional	1994
Davis Cup Records	SINGLES 13-7 DOUBLES 0-0

MARK PHILIPPOUSSIS WAS ONCE asked if he felt more Greek than Australian. "Definitely," he replied. "I feel very close to my Greek heritage. I grew up in a Greek home. We spoke Greek. I spoke Greek before I spoke English."

And so, if Philippoussis's roaring performance in the 2003 Davis Cup Final resonated as much in Athens as it did in Adelaide, that is no great surprise. He and Nick, his father and mentor, speak to each other in their native tongue all the time, and he has that enormous tattoo of Alexander the Great high on his right shoulder.

"I had it put there because of Alexander's Greek blood," Philippoussis said. "He was a conqueror, he was a great fighter. No matter how the odds were stacked against him, he was always fighting. That's what I intend to do with my life."

It all came together for Mark Philippoussis in a manner that showed he can live up to his compatriot's character, and there was no doubting him now. Yet there remains about Philippoussis a sense of innate vulnerability. A former agent of his called him "Speak Softly—wield Big Stick." It is often hard to reconcile the soft-spoken side of him to the overtly physical nature of his tennis game.

He is often found to be delightful company, honest, uncomplicated, as fresh and as free as the waves in which he spends so much of his time. He may have a personality as wide as any ocean, but there is a tranquillity about him, a calmness—almost a remoteness, which has made it difficult for many to get close enough to know exactly what to make of Philippoussis the man.

He is never less than an agreeable, interesting interviewee, who has had his fair share of troubles but does not moan and groan about them. He gets on with life—one that has kicked him where it hurts enough times for only those with hard hearts not to have been thrilled at his contribution to the 2003 campaign.

One minute he will shy away from publicity, the next, as happened at the 1996 Atlanta Olympics, he was in the crowd, bare-chested and face-painted, cheering his compatriots Todd Woodbridge and Mark Woodforde to victory in the men's doubles final. A conundrum is this Philippoussis.

He heartily dislikes one of his nicknames, "Scud," because it evokes the thought that he is all biff-bang and nothing else. True, he does possess enormous strength, but there are times, too, when his tennis bears the other side of his nature: gentle, subtle, and classy.

"Everyone matures differently, in different stages," he said. "I'm definitely a late maturer. I've always liked to have a lot of fun, still do, but I've learned that I need to live by some rules. Having fun is fine, but when you work hard and deserve that fun, then it's a different story. I've really admired the way the Aussie guys like Pat Rafter and Lleyton Hewitt have carried themselves over the years. The job Lleyton's done for someone so young is incredible. Now I think I'm ready for that myself."

And so it has proved. ●

FINAL ROUND

mark philippoussis

117

RESULTS

WORLD GROUP

First Round 7-9 February

France defeated Romania 4-1, Bucharest ROM; Carpet (I):
Sebastien Grosjean (FRA) d. Adrian Voinea (ROM) 62 63 76(10); Nicolas Escude (FRA) d. Andrei Pavel (ROM) 76(2) 62 76(5); Michael Llodra/Fabrice Santoro (FRA) d. Andrei Pavel/Gabriel Trifu (ROM) 64 63 76(4); Victor Hanescu (ROM) d. Fabrice Santoro (FRA) 61 64; Nicolas Escude (FRA) d. Gabriel Trifu (ROM) 76(3) 46 64.

Switzerland defeated Netherlands 3-2, Arnhem NED; Carpet (I):
Sjeng Schalken (NED) d. Michel Kratochvil (SUI) 63 75 16 46 64; Roger Federer (SUI) d. Raemon Sluiter (NED) 62 61 63; Paul Haarhuis/Martin Verkerk (NED) d. George Bastl/Roger Federer (SUI) 36 63 64 75; Roger Federer (SUI) d. Sjeng Schalken (NED) 76(2) 64 75; Michel Kratochvil (SUI) d. Martin Verkerk (NED) 16 76(5) 76(6) 61.

Australia defeated Great Britain 4-1, Sydney AUS; Clay (O):
Mark Philippoussis (AUS) d. Alan Mackin (GBR) 63 63 63; Lleyton Hewitt (AUS) d. Alex Bogdanovic (GBR) 75 61 62; Lleyton Hewitt/Todd Woodbridge (AUS) d. Miles Maclagan/Arvind Parmar (GBR) 61 63 46 62; Wayne Arthurs (AUS) d. Miles Maclagan (GBR) 46 61 64; Alex Bogdanovic (GBR) d. Todd Woodbridge (AUS) 62 76(4).

Sweden defeated Brazil 3-2, Helsingborg SWE; Carpet (I):
Gustavo Kuerten (BRA) d. Andreas Vinciguerra (SWE) 61 64 64; Jonas Bjorkman (SWE) d. Andre Sa (BRA) 64 57 62 46 61; Gustavo Kuerten/Andre Sa (BRA) d. Jonas Bjorkman/Magnus Larsson (SWE) 64 26 57 62 62; Jonas Bjorkman (SWE) d. Gustavo Kuerten (BRA) 64 64 46 46 61; Andreas Vinciguerra (SWE) d. Flavio Saretta (BRA) 61 75 63.

Croatia defeated USA 4-1, Zagreb CRO; Carpet (I):
Ivan Ljubicic (CRO) d. Mardy Fish (USA) 75 63 64; James Blake (USA) d. Mario Ancic (CRO) 61 62 76(5); Goran Ivanisevic/Ivan Ljubicic (CRO) d. James Blake/Mardy Fish (USA) 36 46 76(4) 64 64; Ivan Ljubicic (CRO) d. James Blake (USA) 63 67(5) 64 63; Mario Ancic (CRO) d. Taylor Dent (USA) 76(5) 36 76 (10).

Spain defeated Belgium 5-0, Seville ESP; Clay (O):
Juan Carlos Ferrero (ESP) d. Christophe Rochus (BEL) 63 62 75; Carlos Moya (ESP) d. Xavier Malisse (BEL) 76(2) 61 76(5); Alex Corretja/Albert Costa (ESP) d. Olivier Rochus/Kristof Vliegen (BEL) 64 46 63 36 86; Juan Carlos Ferrero (ESP) d. Kristof Vliegen (BEL) 61 64; Carlos Moya (ESP) d. Christophe Rochus (BEL) 62 62.

Argentina defeated Germany 5-0, Buenos Aires ARG; Clay (O):
Gaston Gaudio (ARG) d. Rainer Schuettler (GER) 62 63 60; David Nalbandian (ARG) d. Lars Burgsmuller (GER) 61 76(4) 75; David Nalbandian/Lucas Arnold (ARG) d. Michael Kohlmann/Rainer Schuettler (GER) 61 06 46 61 62; Juan Ignacio Chela (ARG) d. David Prinosil (GER) 64 61; Gaston Gaudio (ARG) d. Lars Burgsmuller (GER) 63 61.

Russia defeated Czech Republic 3-2, Ostrava CZE; Clay (I):
Jiri Novak (CZE) d. Nikolay Davydenko (RUS) 64 46 61 61; Mikhail Youzhny (RUS) d. Radek Stepanek (CZE) 36 76(8) 67(6) 62 63; Yevgeny Kafelnikov/Mikhail Youzhny (RUS) d. Martin Damm/Cyril Suk (CZE) 76(1) 46 63 63; Jiri Novak (CZE) d. Yevgeny Kafelnikov (RUS) 62 63 76(5); Nikolay Davydenko (RUS) d. Radek Stepanek (CZE) 16 76(4) 62 36 60.

Quarterfinals 4-6 April

Switzerland defeated France 3-2, Toulouse FRA; Carpet (I):
Sebastien Grosjean (FRA) d. George Bastl (SUI) 63 64 36 63; Roger Federer (SUI) d. Nicolas Escude (FRA) 64 75 62; Roger Federer/Marc Rosset (SUI) d. Nicolas Escude/Fabrice Santoro (FRA) 64 36 63 76(4); Roger Federer (SUI) d. Fabrice Santoro (FRA) 61 60 62; Nicolas Escude (FRA) d. George Bastl (SUI) 76(5) 57 76(3).

Australia defeated Sweden 5-0, Malmo SWE; Hard (I):
Mark Philippoussis (AUS) d. Jonas Bjorkman (SWE) 64 63 63; Lleyton Hewitt (AUS) d. Thomas Enqvist (SWE) 64 62 57 64; Wayne Arthurs/Todd Woodbridge (AUS) d. Jonas Bjorkman/Thomas Enqvist (SWE) 64 62 62; Wayne Arthurs (AUS) d. Joachim Johansson (SWE) 63 36 76(4); Mark Philippoussis (AUS) d. Magnus Norman (SWE) 75 57 63.

Spain defeated Croatia 5-0, Valencia ESP; Clay (O): Juan Carlos Ferrero (ESP) d. Mario Ancic (CRO) 64 62 76(1); Carlos Moya (ESP) d. Ivan Ljubicic (CRO) 67(5) 61 64 64; Alex Corretja/Albert Costa (ESP) d. Ivan Ljubicic/Lovro Zovko (CRO) 62 63 64; Albert Costa (ESP) d. Ivan Ljubicic (CRO) 63 64; Alex Corretja (ESP) d. Mario Ancic (CRO) 75 63.

Argentina defeated Russia 5-0, Buenos Aires ARG; Clay (O):
David Nalbandian (ARG) d. Nikolay Davydenko (RUS) 62 62 75; Gaston Gaudio (ARG) d. Yevgeny Kafelnikov (RUS) 64 60 62; Lucas Arnold/David Nalbandian (ARG) d. Yevgeny Kafelnikov/Mikhail Youzhny (RUS) 36 63 64 63; Mariano Zabaleta (ARG) d. Mikhail Youzhny (RUS) 61 64; Gaston Gaudio (ARG) d. Nikolay Davydenko (RUS) 76(4) 63.

Semifinals 19-21 September

Australia defeated Switzerland 3-2, Melbourne, AUS; Hard (O):
Lleyton Hewitt (AUS) d. Michel Kratochvil (SUI) 64 64 61; Roger Federer (SUI) d. Mark Philippoussis (AUS) 63 64 76(3); Wayne Arthurs/Todd Woodbridge (AUS) d. Roger Federer/Marc Rosset (SUI) 46 76(5) 57 64 64; Lleyton Hewitt (AUS) d. Roger Federer (SUI) 57 26 76(4) 75 61; Michel Kratochvil (SUI) d. Todd Woodbridge (AUS) 64 ret.

Spain defeated Argentina 3-2, Malaga, ESP; Clay (O):
Juan Carlos Ferrero (ESP) d. Gaston Gaudio (ARG) 64 60 60; Carlos Moya (ESP) d. Mariano Zabaleta (ARG) 57 26 62 60 61; Lucas Arnold/Agustin Calleri (ARG) d. Alex Corretja/Albert Costa (ESP) 63 16 64 62; Agustin Calleri (ARG) d. Juan Carlos Ferrero (ESP) 64 75 61; Carlos Moya (ESP) d. Gaston Gaudio (ARG) 61 64 62.

Final 28-30 December

Australia defeated Spain 3-1, Melbourne AUS; Grass (O):
Lleyton Hewitt (AUS) d. Juan Carlos Ferrero (ESP) 36 63 36 76(0) 62; Carlos Moya (ESP) d. Mark Philippoussis (AUS) 64 64 46 76(4); Wayne Arthurs/Todd Woodbridge (AUS) d. Alex Corretja/Feliciano Lopez (ESP) 63 61 63; Mark Philippoussis (AUS) d. Juan Carlos Ferrero (ESP) 75 63 16 26 60; Lleyton Hewitt (AUS) vs Carlos Moya (ESP) not played.

World Group Play-offs 19-21 September

Austria defeated Belgium 3-2, Portschach, AUT; Clay (O):
Stefan Koubek (AUT) d. Christophe Rochus (BEL) 62 64 61; Jurgen Melzer (AUT) d. Olivier Rochus (BEL) 61 76(4) 57 26 61; Olivier Rochus/Kristof Vliegen (BEL) d. Julian Knowle/Alexander Peya (AUT) 46 61 64 62; Stefan Koubek (AUT) d. Olivier Rochus (BEL) 67(4) 62 75 46 63; Kristof Vliegen (BEL) d. Jurgen Melzer (AUT) 75 64.

Canada defeated Brazil 3-2, Calgary, CAN; Carpet (I):
Flavio Saretta (BRA) d. Frederic Niemeyer (CAN) 64 76(5) 67(4) 64; Daniel Nestor (CAN) d. Gustavo Kuerten (BRA) 67(7) 76(0) 63 67(7) 75; Daniel Nestor/Frederic Niemeyer (CAN) d. Gustavo Kuerten/Andre Sa (BRA) 63 62 16 62; Gustavo Kuerten (BRA) d. Simon Larose (CAN) 76(4) 76(4) 36 76(10); Frank Dancevic (CAN) d. Flavio Saretta (BRA) 63 75 36 76(7).

Czech Republic defeated Thailand 4-1, Bangkok, THA; Hard (I):
Jiri Novak (CZE) d. Danai Udomchoke (THA) 62 62 76(1); Paradorn Srichaphan (THA) d. Bohdan Ulihrach (CZE) 76(2) 62 76(4); Tomas Berdych/Jiri Novak (CZE) d. Paradorn Srichaphan/Danai Udomchoke (THA) 63 76(2) 64; Jiri Novak (CZE) d. Paradorn Srichaphan (THA) 64 64 64; Tomas Berdych (CZE) d. Danai Udomchoke (THA) 76(2) 63.

Belarus defeated Germany 3-2, Sundern, GER; Clay (O):
Max Mirnyi (BLR) d. Tomas Behrend (GER) 57 26 76(6) 62 64; Rainer Schuettler (GER) d. Vladimir Voltchkov (BLR) 63 36 67(3) 64 64; Max Mirnyi/Vladimir Voltchkov (BLR) d. Nicolas Kiefer/Rainer Schuettler (GER) 63 36 75 75; Max Mirnyi (BLR) d. Rainer Schuettler (GER) 63 75 63; Lars Burgsmuller (GER) d. Alexander Skrypko (BLR) 62 60.

Morocco defeated Great Britain 3-2, Casablanca, MAR; Clay (O):
Hicham Arazi (MAR) d. Tim Henman (GBR) 64 64 76(4); Younes El Aynaoui (MAR) d. Greg Rusedski (GBR) 36 63 64 36 61; Tim Henman/Greg Rusedski (GBR) d. Hicham Arazi/Mounir El Aarej (MAR) 76(3) 62 64; Tim Henman (GBR) d. Younes El Aynaoui (MAR) 63 67(4) 76(5) 64; Hicham Arazi (MAR) d. Greg Rusedski (GBR) 57 75 76(7) 76(5).

Netherlands defeated India 5-0, Zwolle, NED; Carpet (I):
Martin Verkerk (NED) d. Rohan Bopanna (IND) 57 63 57 76(7) 1210; Sjeng Schalken (NED) d. Prakash Amritraj (IND) 63 61 61; John Van Lottum/Martin Verkerk (NED) d. Mahesh Bhupathi/Rohan Bopanna (IND) 46 75 75 64; Sjeng Schalken (NED) d. Harsh Mankad (IND) 63 61; Raemon Sluiter (NED) d. Prakash Amritraj (IND) 61 63.

Romania defeated Ecuador 3-2, Quito, ECU; Clay (O):
Victor Hanescu (ROM) d. Giovanni Lapentti (ECU) 76(3) 67(5) 76(5) 67(1) 64; Nicolas Lapentti (ECU) d. Razvan Sabau (ROM) 62 64 36 46 63; Florin Mergea/Horia Tecau (ROM) d. Giovanni Lapentti/Nicolas Lapentti (ECU) 76(2) 16 63 36 1311; Nicolas Lapentti (ECU) d. Victor Hanescu (ROM) 64 67(4) 67(5) 76(13) 63; Razvan Sabau (ROM) d. Giovanni Lapentti (ECU) 64 36 64 57 75.

USA defeated Slovak Republic 3-2, Bratislava, SVK; Clay (O):
Dominik Hrbaty (SVK) d. Andy Roddick (USA) 36 63 64 64; Mardy Fish (USA) d. Karol Kucera (SVK) 46 75 75 61; Bob Bryan/Mike Bryan (USA) d. Karol Beck/Dominik Hrbaty (SVK) 61 64 76(5); Andy Roddick (USA) d. Karol Beck (SVK) 63 64 64; Michal Mertinak (SVK) d. Mardy Fish (USA) 36 63 64.

GROUP I

Euro/African Zone
First Round 7-9 February

Slovak Republic – bye. Luxembourg – bye. Finland – bye.

Austria defeated Norway 5-0, Oslo NOR; Hard (I): Jurgen Melzer (AUT) d. Stian Boretti (NOR) 62 62 61; Alexander Peya (AUT) d. Jan Frode Andersen (NOR) 63 63 75; Jurgen Melzer/Alexander Peya (AUT) d. Jan Frode Andersen/Stian Boretti (NOR) 63 62 67(4) 46 75; Oliver Marach (AUT) d. Fredrik Aarum (NOR) 64 62; Konstantin Gruber (AUT) d. Stian Boretti (NOR) 63 75.

Belarus defeated Israel 3-2, Minsk BLR; Carpet (I): Max Mirnyi (BLR) d. Harel Levy (ISR) 61 67(2) 63 76(6); Vladimir Voltchkov (BLR) d. Noam Okun (ISR) 62 76(5) 63; Max Mirnyi/Vladimir Voltchkov (BLR) d. Jonathan Erlich/Andy Ram (ISR) 76(2) 64 64; Andy Ram (ISR) d. Alexander Shvec (BLR) 61 32 ret.; Harel Levy (ISR) d. Alexander Skrypko (BLR) 64 64.

Zimbabwe – bye. Italy – bye. Morocco – bye.

Second Round 4-6 April

Slovak Republic defeated Luxembourg 3-2, Esch/Alzette LUX; Hard (I): Gilles Muller (LUX) d. Michal Mertinak (SVK) 75 63 76(6); Karol Beck (SVK) d. Gilles Kremer (LUX) 63 64 62; Gilles Muller/Mike Scheidweiler (LUX) d. Karol Beck/Igor Zelenay (SVK) 75 75 64; Karol Beck (SVK) d. Gilles Muller (LUX) 64 63 63; Michal Mertinak (SVK) d. Mike Scheidweiler (LUX) 46 63 62 64.

Austria defeated Finland 3-2, St. Anton AUT; Hard (I):
Stefan Koubek (AUT) d. Tuomas Ketola (FIN) 75 46 76(3) 61; Jarkko Nieminen (FIN) d. Jurgen Melzer (AUT) 76(5) 46 64 46 64; Julian Knowle/Alexander Peya (AUT) d. Tuomas Ketola/Jarkko Nieminen (FIN) 26 64 76(4) 75; Jarkko Nieminen (FIN) d. Stefan Koubek (AUT) 63 62 63; Jurgen Melzer (AUT) d. Tuomas Ketola (FIN) 76(2) 36 67(6) 62 62.

Belarus defeated Zimbabwe 4-1, Minsk BLR; Carpet (I):
Max Mirnyi (BLR) d. Kevin Ullyett (ZIM) 76(4) 64; Vladimir Voltchkov (BLR) d. Wayne Black (ZIM) 67(4) 64 62 75; Max Mirnyi/Vladimir Voltchkov (BLR) d. Wayne Black/Kevin Ullyett (ZIM) 57 63 75 76(4); Alexander Skrypko (BLR) d. Wayne Black (ZIM) 63 63; Gwinyai Tongoona (ZIM) d. Vladimir Voltchkov (BLR) 16 21 ret.

Morocco defeated Italy 3-2, Marrakech MAR; Clay (O):
Younes El Aynaoui (MAR) d. Filippo Volandri (ITA) 76(6) 64 36 76(5); Davide Sanguinetti (ITA) d. Hicham Arazi (MAR) 75 16 06 64 63; Massimo Bertolini/Giorgio Galimberti (ITA) d. Mounir El Aarej/Younes El Aynaoui (MAR) 61 64 61; Younes El Aynaoui (MAR) d. Davide Sanguinetti (ITA) 64 63 62; Hicham Arazi (MAR) d. Filippo Volandri (ITA) 63 63 62.

Slovak Republic, Austria, Belarus and Morocco advanced to World Group Play-offs on 19-21 September 2003

Second Round/Play-off 11-13 July

Finland defeated Norway 4-1; Asker NOR; Clay (O):
Jarkko Nieminen (FIN) d. Stian Boretti (NOR) 61 51 ret.; Jan-Frode Andersen (NOR) d. Janne Ojala (FIN) 46 63 76(3) 75; Tuomas Ketola/Jarkko Nieminen (FIN) d. Jan-Frode Andersen/Stian Boretti (NOR) 75 64 64; Jarkko Nieminen (FIN) d. Jan-Frode Andersen (NOR) 62 62 64; Kim Tiilikainen (FIN) d. Thomas Haug (NOR) 61 63.

Israel defeated Zimbabwe 5-0, Ramat Hasharon ISR; Clay (O):
Noam Okun (ISR) d. Gwinyai Tongoona (ZIM) 64 63 64; Harel Levy (ISR) d. Genius Chidzikwe (ZIM) 62 64 64; Jonathan Erlich/Andy Ram (ISR) d. Genius Chidzikwe/Gwinyai Chingoka (ZIM) 75 64 64; Noam Okun (ISR) d. Zibusiso Ncube (ZIM) 64 76(3); Jonathan Erlich (ISR) d. Gwinyai Chingoka (ZIM) 64 60.

Third Round/Play-off 19-21 September

Luxembourg defeated Norway 5-0, Asker, NOR; Clay (O):
Gilles Muller (LUX) d. Stian Boretti (NOR) 63 76(3) 26 63; Mike Scheidweiler (LUX) d. Jan-Frode Andersen (NOR) 64 64 76(4); Gilles Muller/Mike Scheidweiler (LUX) d. Jan-Frode Andersen/Stian Boretti (NOR) 61 46 36 63 64; Gilles Kremer (LUX) d. Helge Koll-Frafjord (NOR) 64 ret; Laurent Hild (LUX) d. Erling Tveit (NOR) 63 67(5) 63.

Zimbabwe defeated Italy 3-2, Harare, ZIM; Hard (O):
Kevin Ullyett (ZIM) d. Filippo Volandri (ITA) 46 75 63 76(5); Wayne Black (ZIM) d. Davide Sanguinetti (ITA) 76(2) 61 63; Wayne Black/Kevin Ullyett (ZIM) d. Massimo Bertolini/Giorgio Galimberti (ITA) 76(7) 62 64; Giorgio Galimberti (ITA) d. Genius Chidzikwe (ZIM) 62 62; Davide Sanguinetti (ITA) d. Nigel Badza (ZIM) 61 61.

Norway and Italy relegated to Europe/Africa Zone Group II in 2004

American Zone
First Round 7-9 February

Venezuela – bye.

Ecuador defeated Chile 3-2, Quito ECU; Clay (O); Nicolas Lapentti (ECU) d. Hermes Gamonal (CHI) 62 61 76(1); Giovanni Lapentti (ECU) d. Marcelo Rios (CHI) 63 76(5) 63; Hermes Gamonal/Adrian Garcia (CHI) d. Giovanni Lapentti/Nicolas Lapentti (ECU) 26 46 76(3) 64 63; Marcelo Rios (CHI) d. Nicolas Lapentti (ECU) 36 64 76(0) 76(5); Giovanni Lapentti (ECU) d. Hermes Gamonal (CHI) 76(4) 64 67(4) 63.

Peru defeated Bahamas 5-0, Lima PER; Clay (O): Ivan Miranda (PER) d. Mark Knowles (BAH) 64 36 61 ret.; Luis Horna (PER) d. Mark Merklein (BAH) 62 61 63; Luis Horna/Ivan Miranda (PER) d. Mark Merklein/Bjorn Munroe (BAH) 64 64 76(4); Mario Monroy (PER) d. Marvin Rolle (BAH) 64 46 75; Willy Lock (PER) d. Bjorn Munroe (BAH) 61 63.

Canada – bye.

Second Round 4-6 April

Ecuador defeated Venezuela 3-2, Salinas ECU; Clay (O):
Jose De Armas (VEN) d. Giovanni Lapentti (ECU) 67(4) 26 76(4) ret; Nicolas Lapentti (ECU) d. Kepler Orellana (VEN) 64 63 46 55 ret; Giovanni Lapentti/Nicolas Lapentti (ECU) d. Jose De Armas/Kepler Orellana (VEN) 61 63 63; Nicolas Lapentti (ECU) d. Jose De Armas (VEN) 36 64 63 63; Jhonathan Medina-Alvarez (VEN) d. Carlos Avellan (ECU) 63 62;

Canada defeated Peru 5-0, Calgary CAN; Hard (I): Daniel Nestor (CAN) d. Ivan Miranda (PER) 62 62 36 64; Frank Dancevic (CAN) d. Diego Acuna (PER) 46 76(3) 36 63 86; Simon Larose/Daniel Nestor (CAN) d. Diego Acuna/Ivan Miranda (PER) 76(6) 63 67(5) 46 63; Matt Klinger (CAN) d. William Lock (PER) 76(4) 76(7); Simon Larose (CAN) d. Juan-Carlos Rebaza-Lozano (PER) 60 61.

Ecuador and Canada advanced to World Group Play-offs on 19-21 September 2003.

Second Round/Play-off 11-13 July

Chile defeated Venezuela 3-2, Caracas VEN; Hard (O):
Fernando Gonzalez (CHI) d. Kepler Orellana (VEN) 64 62 75; Jose De Armas (VEN) d. Marcelo Rios (CHI) 75 62 36 36 86; Hermes Gamonal/Fernando Gonzalez (CHI) d. Jose De Armas/Kepler Orellana (VEN) 75 64 64; Fernando Gonzalez (CHI) d. Jose De Armas (VEN) 64 64 64; Kepler Orellana (VEN) d. Marcelo Rios (CHI) 76(4) ret.

RESULTS

RESULTS

Third Round/Play-off 19-21 September

Venezuela defeated Bahamas 4-0, Maracaibo, VEN; Hard (O):
Kepler Orellana (VEN) d. Devin Mullings (BAH) 63 61 61; Jose De Armas (VEN) d. Christopher Eldon (BAH) 64 64 75; Jose De Armas/Kepler Orellana (VEN) d. Christopher Eldon/Devin Mullings (BAH) 60 64 61; Jhonathan Medina-Alvarez (VEN) d. Davin Russell (BAH) 61 61; Kepler Orellana (VEN) vs Christopher Eldon (BAH) not played.

Bahamas relegated to Americas Zone Group II in 2004

Asia/Oceania Zone
First Round 7-9 February

India defeated Japan 4-1, New Delhi IND; Grass (O):
Gouichi Motomura (JPN) d. Rohan Bopanna (IND) 64 67(4) 76(4) 63; Leander Paes (IND) d. Takao Suzuki (JPN) 63 76(3) 64; Mahesh Bhupathi/Leander Paes (IND) d. Jun Kato/Thomas Shimada (JPN) 62 62 63; Rohan Bopanna (IND) d. Jun Kato (JPN) 76(5) 64 64; Leander Paes (IND) d. Gouichi Motomura (JPN) 16 63 64.

New Zealand defeated Pakistan 5-0, Hamilton NZL; Hard (O):
Mark Nielsen (NZL) d. Aqeel Khan (PAK) 60 61 62; Alistair Hunt (NZL) d. Aisam Qureshi (PAK) 64 16 75 62; Alistair Hunt/Mark Nielsen (NZL) d. Aqeel Khan/Aisam Qureshi (PAK) 63 61 67(4) 75; James Shortall (NZL) d. Asim Shafik (PAK) 62 62; Robert Cheyne (NZL) d. Nomi Qamar (PAK) 62 60.

Uzbekistan defeated Indonesia 3-2, Tashkent UZB; Clay (O):
Oleg Ogorodov (UZB) d. Peter Handoyo (INA); 76(6) 57 64 57 63; Febi Widhiyanto (INA) d. Vadim Kutsenko (UZB) 26 76(5) 62 06 62; Peter Handoyo/Suwandi Suwandi (INA) d. Vadim Kutsenko/Oleg Ogorodov (UZB) 76(2) 63 57 64; Vadim Kutsenko (UZB) d. Peter Handoyo (INA) 46 64 61 60; Oleg Ogorodov (UZB) d. Febi Widhiyanto (INA) 16 75 75 60.

Thailand defeated Korea 4-1, Bangkok THA; Carpet (I):
Paradorn Srichaphan (THA) d. Hee-Seok Chung (KOR) 62 62 63; Danai Udomchoke (THA) d. Dong-Hyun Kim (KOR) 63 57 61 62; Hee-Seok Chung/Hee-Sung Chung (KOR) d. Attapol Rithiwattanapong/Narathorn Srichaphan (THA) 61 64 61; Paradorn Srichaphan (THA) d. Dong-Hyun Kim (KOR) 63 64 76(3); Danai Udomchoke (THA) d. Hee-Seok Chung (KOR) 61 63.

Second Round 4-6 April

India defeated New Zealand 4-1, Kolkata IND; Grass (O):
Leander Paes (IND) d. Mark Nielsen (NZL) 61 76(1) 62; Alistair Hunt (NZL) d. Rohan Bopanna (IND) 46 46 63 62 97; Mahesh Bhupathi/Leander Paes (IND) d. Alistair Hunt/Mark Nielsen (NZL) 63 62 62; Rohan Bopanna (IND) d. James Shortall (NZL) 63 62 64; Leander Paes (IND) d. Robert Cheyne (NZL) 61 60.

Thailand defeated Uzbekistan 4-1, Tashkent UZB; Hard (I):
Danai Udomchoke (THA) d. Vadim Kutsenko (UZB) 62 62 63; Paradorn Srichaphan (THA) d. Oleg Ogorodov (UZB) 63 64 64; Vadim Kutsenko/Oleg Ogorodov (UZB) d. Attapol Rithiwattanapong/Narathorn Srichaphan (THA) 41 ret; Paradorn Srichaphan (THA) d. Vadim Kutsenko (UZB) 63 63; Danai Udomchoke (THA) d. Murad Inoyatov (UZB) 64 63.

India and Thailand advanced to World Group Play-offs on 19-21 September 2003

Second Round/Play-off 4-6 April

Japan defeated Pakistan 5-0, Toyota JPN; Hard (I):
Gouichi Motomura (JPN) d. Shahzad Khan (PAK) 62 63 61; Takao Suzuki (JPN) d. Aqeel Khan (PAK) 61 61 64; Thomas Shimada/Takahiro Terachi (JPN) d. Aqeel Khan/Shahzad-Samad Khan (PAK) 61 61 60; Gouichi Motomura (JPN) d. Inam Gul (PAK) 60 61; Takao Suzuki (JPN) d. Shahzad Khan (PAK) 62 62.

Indonesia defeated Korea, Rep. 3-2, Surabaya INA; Hard (O):
Febi Widhiyanto (INA) d. Dong-Hyun Kim (KOR) 61 63 60; Hee-Seok Chung (KOR) d. Peter Handoyo (INA) 75 62 21 ret; Peter Handoyo/Suwandi Suwandi (INA) d. Hee-Seok Chung/Hee-Sung Chung (KOR) 75 64 64; Suwandi Suwandi (INA) d. Kyu-Tae Im (KOR) 64 64 61; Hee-Seok Chung (KOR) d. Prima Simpatiaji (INA) 75 76(2).

Third Round/Play-off 19-21 September

Pakistan defeated Korea, Rep. 3-2; Lahore, PAK; Grass (O):
Aisam Qureshi (PAK) d. Kyu-Tae Im (KOR) 61 62 64; Young-Joon Kim (KOR) d. Aqeel Khan (PAK) 76(17) 46 63 76(8); Aqeel Khan/Aisam Qureshi (PAK) d. Hee-Seok Chung/Hee-Sung Chung (KOR) 64 64 64; Young-Joon Kim (KOR) d. Aisam Qureshi (PAK) 67(4) 76(5) 67(2) 76(5) 64; Aqeel Khan (PAK) d. Kyu-Tae Im (KOR) 63 63 64.

Korea, Rep. relegated to Asia/Oceania Zone Group II in 2004

GROUP II

Euro/African Zone
First Round 4-6 April

Portugal defeated Monaco 4-1, Maia POR; Clay (O):
Bernardo Mota (POR) d. Emmanuel Heussner (MON) 75 64 63; Emanuel Couto (POR) d. Guillaume Couillard (MON) 75 67(2) 63 61; Emanuel Couto/Bernardo Mota (POR) d. Guillaume Couillard/Emmanuel Heussner (MON) 36 76(7) 62 26 62; Helder Lopes (POR) d. Guillaume Couillard (MON) 75 67(7) 76(2); Emmanuel Heussner (MON) d. Leonardo Tavares (POR) 62 64.

South Africa defeated Poland 3-2, Polokwane RSA; Hard (O):
Rik De Voest (RSA) d. Lukasz Kubot (POL) 36 61 63 60; Wesley Moodie (RSA) d. Mariusz Fyrstenberg (POL) 61 62 62; David Adams/Robbie Koenig (RSA) d. Mariusz Fyrstenberg/Marcin Matkowski (POL) 46 64 62 64; Lukasz Kubot (POL) d. Wesley Moodie (RSA) 64 26 63; Bartlomiej Dabrowski (POL) d. Rik De Voest (RSA) 60 64.

Slovenia defeated Ghana 4-1, Accra GHA; Hard (O):
Andrej Kracman (SLO) d. Salifu Mohammed (GHA) 64 64 16 67(3) 86; Gunther Darkey (GHA) d. Bostjan Osabnik (SLO) 64 61 62; Andrej Kracman/Marko Tkalec (SLO) d. Kwasi Ahenkora/Gunther Darkey (GHA) 75 64 64; Marko Tkalec (SLO) d. Gunther Darkey (GHA) 63 64 76(5); Bostjan Osabnik (SLO) d. Salifu Mohammed (GHA) 62 61.

Denmark defeated Tunisia 4-1, Hillerod DEN; Hard (I): Oualid Jalali (TUN) d. Rasmus Norby (DEN) 06 64 63 16 62; Kenneth Carlsen (DEN) d. Heithem Abid (TUN) 62 61 63; Kenneth Carlsen/Jonathan Printzlau (DEN) d. Oualid Jalali/Malek Jaziri (TUN) 63 64 67(4) 36 86; Kenneth Carlsen (DEN) d. Oualid Jalali (TUN) 63 64 60; Frederik Nielsen (DEN) d. Malek Jaziri (TUN) 61 64.

Bulgaria defeated Ukraine 3-2, Sofia BUL; Carpet (I):
Orest Tereshchuk (UKR) d. Ivaylo Traykov (BUL) 76(2) 67(4) 36 76(6) 64; Radoslav Lukaev (BUL) d. Andrey Dernovskiy (UKR) 63 67(6) 63 62; Todor Enev/Radoslav Lukaev (BUL) d. Andrey Dernovskiy/Orest Tereshchuk (UKR) 63 64 64; Orest Tereshchuk (UKR) d. Radoslav Lukaev (BUL) 36 63 76(7) 63; Ivaylo Traykov (BUL) d. Andrei Stepanov (UKR) 76(3) 64 76(3).

Yugoslavia defeated Cote D'Ivoire 4-1, Belgrade YUG; Carpet (I):
Valentin Sanon (CIV) d. Janko Tipsarevic (YUG) 46 63 63 36 62; Dusan Vemic (YUG) d. Claude N'Goran (CIV) 64 67(6) 64 75; Dusan Vemic/Nenad Zimonjic (YUG) d. Claude N'Goran/Valentin Sanon (CIV) 75 63 64; Janko Tipsarevic (YUG) d. Claude N'Goran (CIV) 62 63 75; Ilija Bozoljac (YUG) d. Jean-Christophe Nabi (CIV) 64 62.

Ireland defeated Egypt 4-1, Dublin IRE; Hard (O): Mohamed Maamoun (EGY) d. Stephen Nugent (IRL) 64 67(4) 63 64; John Doran (IRL) d. Amro Ghoneim (EGY) 36 76(5) 61 63; John Doran/David J. Mullins (IRL) d. Karim Maamoun/Mohamed Maamoun (EGY) 75 61 62; John Doran (IRL) d. Mohamed Maamoun (EGY) 76(3) 63 75; Sean Cooper (IRL) d. Karim Maamoun (EGY) 63 36 62.

Greece defeated Andorra 4-1, Andorra La Vella AND; Carpet (I):
Vasilis Mazarakis (GRE) d. Kenneth Tuilier-Curco (AND) 61 60 61; Konstantinos Economidis (GRE) d. Joan Jimenez-Guerra (AND) 64 64 63; Konstantinos Economidis/Vasilis Mazarakis (GRE) d. Paul Gerbaud-Farras/Joan Jimenez-Guerra (AND) 62 62 36 46 64; Nikos Rovas (GRE) d. Joan Jimenez-Guerra (AND) 36 64 63; Marc Vilanova (AND) d. Alexander Jakupovic (GRE) w/o.

Second Round 11-13 July

South Africa defeated Portugal 5-0, Durban RSA; Hard (O):
Rik De Voest (RSA) d. Helder Lopes (POR) 76(3) 61 64; Wesley Moodie (RSA) d. Leonardo Tavares (POR) 63 64 16 76(7); Chris Haggard/Robbie Koenig (RSA) d. Leonardo Tavares/Rui Machado (POR) 75 63 62; Wesley Moodie (RSA) d. Rui Machado (POR) 26 61 62; Rik De Voest (RSA) d. Leonardo Tavares (POR) 61 64.

Denmark defeated Slovenia 4-1, Hornbaek DEN; Hard (O):
Kenneth Carlsen (DEN) d. Bostjan Osabnik (SLO) 64 75 64; Marko Tkalec (SLO) d. Mik Ledvonova (DEN) 64 57 64 36 63; Kenneth Carlsen/Jonathan Printzlau (DEN) d. Bostjan Osabnik/Rok Jarc (SLO) 63 64 67(4) 61; Kenneth Carlsen (DEN) d. Marko Tkalec (SLO) 62 62 64; Mik Ledvonova (DEN) d. Nejc Podkrajsek (SLO) 16 62 60.

Yugoslavia defeated Bulgaria 4-1, Belgrade YUG; Clay (O):
Janko Tipsarevic (YUG) d. Ilia Kushev (BUL) 63 16 62 63; Radoslav Lukaev (BUL) d. Boris Pashanski (YUG) 36 64 67(3) 64 64; Dejan Petrovic/Nenad Zimonjic (YUG) d. Todor Enev/Radoslav Lukaev (BUL) 63 61 62; Janko Tipsarevic (YUG) d. Radoslav Lukaev (BUL) 63 61 63; Boris Pashanski (YUG) d. Todor Enev (BUL) 62 64.

Greece defeated Ireland 5-0, Athens GRE; Clay (O): Konstantinos Economidis (GRE) d. Peter Clarke (IRL) 76(2) 63 64; Vasilis Mazarakis (GRE) d. Conor Niland (IRL) 62 26 67(1) 61 63; Konstantinos Economidis/Vasilis Mazarakis (GRE) d. John Doran/David J. Mullins (IRL) 62 75 61; Nikos Rovas (GRE) d. John Doran (IRL) 46 54 ret.; Solon Peppas (GRE) d. Conor Niland (IRL) 63 46 64.

Third Round 19-21 September

South Africa defeated Denmark 3-2, Bronby, DEN; Carpet (I):
Wayne Ferreira (RSA) d. Frederik Fetterlein (DEN) 61 61 76(3); Kenneth Carlsen (DEN) d. Wesley Moodie (RSA) 67(1) 76(3) 63 64; Wayne Ferreira/Chris Haggard (RSA) d. Kenneth Carlsen/Frederik Fetterlein (DEN) 63 75 76(5); Kenneth Carlsen (DEN) d. Wayne Ferreira (RSA) 61 76(5) 62; Wesley Moodie (RSA) d. Frederik Nielsen (DEN) 64 64 64.

Greece defeated Yugoslavia 3-2, Athens, GRE; Clay (O):
Janko Tipsarevic (YUG) d. Solon Peppas (GRE) 36 63 62 26 63; Konstantinos Economidis (GRE) d. Boris Pashanski (YUG) 62 64 62; Elefterios Alexiou/Alexander Jakupovic (GRE) d. Dejan Petrovic/Nenad Zimonjic (YUG) 67(6) 63 62 64; Konstantinos Economidis (GRE) d. Janko Tipsarevic (YUG) 60 76(6) 64; Boris Pashanski (YUG) d. Alexander Jakupovic (GRE) 64 63.

South Africa and Greece promoted to Europe/Africa Zone Group I in 2004

Play-off 11-13 July

Poland defeated Monaco 5-0, Gdynia POL; Clay (O):
Mariusz Fyrstenberg (POL) d. Emmanuel Heussner (MON) 64 67(3) 63 61; Bartlomiej Dabrowski (POL) d. Guillaume Couillard (MON) 64 63 62; Marcin Matkowski/Radoslav Nijaki (POL) d. Guillaume Couillard/Emmanuel Heussner (MON) 76(3) 64 63; Radoslav Nijaki (POL) d. Guillaume Couillard (MON) 64 67(6) 62; Marcin Matkowski (POL) d. Emmanuel Heussner (MON) 46 63 64.

Tunisia defeated Ghana 4-1, Tunis TUN; Clay (O): Heithem Abid (TUN) d. Gunther Darkey (GHA) 76(2) 75 26 64; Oualid Jalali (TUN) d. Salifu Mohammed (GHA) 60 62 61; Oualid Jalali/Issam Jallali (TUN) d. Gunther Darkey/Samuel-Etse Fumi (GHA) 64 75 63; Oualid Jalali (TUN) d. Kwasi Ahenkora (GHA) 64 60; Salifu Mohammed (GHA) d. Tarek Ben Soltane (TUN) 26 75 63.

Ukraine defeated Cote D'Ivoire 3-2, Kakhovka UKR; Clay (O):
Claude N'Goran (CIV) d. Nikolay Dyachok (UKR) 64 62 62; Orest Tereshchuk (UKR) d. Valentin Sanon (CIV) 61 63 63; Andrey Dernovskiy/Orest Tereshchuk (UKR) d. Claude N'Goran/Valentin Sanon (CIV) 63 62 62; Claude N'Goran (CIV) d. Orest Tereshchuk (UKR) 64 62 64; Sergei Yaroshenko (UKR) d. Valentin Sanon (CIV) 46 64 26 63 63.

Egypt defeated Andorra 3-2, Andorra La Vella AND; Carpet (I):
Joan Jimenez-Guerra (AND) d. Mohamed Maamoun (EGY) 63 36 63 76(3); Karim Maamoun (EGY) d. Kenneth Tuilier-Curco (AND) 62 60 67(0) 61; Amro Ghoneim/Mohamed Maamoun (EGY) d. Paul Gerbaud-Farras/Joan Jimenez-Guerra (AND) 57 76(5) 64 64; Karim Maamoun (EGY) d. Joan Jimenez-Guerra (AND) 46 76(2) 67(6) 64 86; Paul Gerbaud-Farras (AND) d. Mohamed Fawzy (EGY) 76(4) 64.

Monaco, Ghana, Cote D'Ivoire and Andorra relegated to Europe/Africa Zone III in 2004

American Zone
First Round 7-9 February

Mexico defeated Netherlands Antilles 5-0, Aguascalientes MEX; Carpet (I): Miguel Galladro (MEX) d. Kevin Jonckheer (AHO) 64 64 64; Luis Manuel Flores (MEX) d. Elmar Gerth (AHO) 62 60 62; Guillermo Carter/Bruno Echagary (MEX) d. Piet Hein Boekel/Elmar Gerth (AHO) 75 64 63; Guillermo Carter (MEX) d. Piet Hein Boekel (AHO) 67(3) 62 60; Luis Manuel Flores (MEX) d. Leroy Tujeehut (AHO) 61 61.

Paraguay defeated Haiti 5-0, Paraguayo PAR; Carpet (O):
Francisco Rodriguez (PAR) d. Jerry Joseph (HAI) 61 63 60; Paulo Carvallo (PAR) d. Iphton Louis (HAI) 60 67(7) 64 26 61; Paulo Carvallo/Francisco Rodriguez (PAR) d. Joel Allen/Iphton Louis (HAI) 76(3) 61 76(7); Gustavo Ramirez (PAR) d. Joel Allen (HAI) 60 62; Emilio Baez-Britez (PAR) d. Jerry Joseph (HAI) 60 61.

Cuba defeated Colombia 5-0, Havana CUB; Hard (O):
Ricardo Chile (CUB) d. Carlos Salamanca (COL) 64 63 64; Lazaro Navarro-Batles (CUB) d. Daniel Isaza (COL) 62 76(1) 61; Sandor Martinez-Breijo/Lazaro Navarro-Batles (CUB) d. Daniel Isaza/Carlos Salamanca (COL) 76(6) 61 36 63; Eddy Gonzalez (CUB) d. Carlos Salamanca (COL) 64 75; Sandor Martinez-Breijo (CUB) d. Daniel Isaza (COL) 64 62.

Dominican Republic defeated Uruguay 4-1, Maldonado URU; Clay (O): Johnson Garcia (DOM) d. Marcel Felder (URU) 63 76(3) 75; Victor Estrella (DOM) d. Martin Vilarrubi (URU) 57 64 64 64; Victor Estrella/Johnson Garcia (DOM) d. Marcel Felder/Martin Vilarrubi (URU) 67(4) 64 64 64; Marcel Felder (URU) d. Jose Bernard (DOM) 60 62; Johnson Garcia (DOM) d. Martin Vilarrubi (URU) 62 64.

Second Round 4-6 April

Paraguay defeated Mexico 4-1, Asuncion PAR; Clay (O):
Paulo Carvallo (PAR) d. Miguel Gallardo-Valles (MEX) 61 76(4) 64; Francisco Rodriguez (PAR) d. Bruno Echagaray (MEX) 60 62 26 06 61; Paulo Carvallo/Francisco Rodriguez (PAR) d. Bruno Echagaray/Santiago Gonzalez (MEX) 61 16 06 62 62; Francisco Rodriguez (PAR) d. Miguel Gallardo-Valles (MEX) 21 ret; Santiago Gonzalez (MEX) d. Ricardo Mena (PAR) 64 46 62.

Dominican Republic defeated Cuba 4-1, Santo Domingo DOM; Clay (O): Victor Estrella (DOM) d. Ricardo Chile-Fonte (CUB) 62 62 63; Johnson Garcia (DOM) d. Lazaro Navarro-Batles (CUB) 64 64 75; Victor Estrella/Johnson Garcia (DOM) d. Sandor Martinez-Breijo/Lazaro Navarro-Batles (CUB) 76(4) 76(5) 63; Jose Bernard (DOM) d. Sandor Martinez-Breijo (CUB) 62 62; Ricardo Chile-Fonte (CUB) d. Jose Antonio Velazquez (DOM) 60 61.

Third Round 19-21 September

Paraguay defeated Dominican Republic 4-1, Santo Domingo, DOM; Hard (O): Victor Estrella (DOM) d. Francisco Rodriguez (PAR) 46 26 61 64 64; Ramon Delgado (PAR) d. Johnson Garcia (DOM) 61 62 64; Paulo Carvallo/Ramon Delgado (PAR) d. Victor Estrella/Johnson Garcia (DOM) 62 63 64; Ramon Delgado (PAR) d. Victor Estrella (DOM) 62 62 61; Francisco Rodriguez (PAR) d. Johnson Garcia (DOM) 64 64.

Paraguay promoted to Americas Zone Group I in 2004

Play-off 4-6 April

Haiti defeated Netherlands Antilles 3-2, Willemstad AHO; Hard (O): Iphton Louis (HAI) d. Elmar Gerth (AHO) 64 64 61; Jean-Julien Rojer (AHO) d. Bertrand Madsen (HAI) 63 75 60; Iphton Louis/Bertrand Madsen (HAI) d. Kevin Jonckheer/Jean-Julien Rojer (AHO) 76(3) 57 64 36 63; Jean-Julien Rojer (AHO) d. Iphton Louis (HAI) 61 62 63; Bertrand Madsen (HAI) d. Raoul Behr (AHO) 61 67(5) 76(5) 62.

Uruguay defeated Colombia 3-2, Montevideo URU; Clay (O):
Federico Dondo (URU) d. Pablo Gonzalez (COL) 64 62 61; Michael Quintero (COL) d. Martin Vilarrubi (URU) 60 64 67(5) 61; Marcel Felder/Martín Vilarrubi (URU) d. Pablo Gonzalez/Michael Quintero (COL) 63 60 63; Michael Quintero (COL) d. Federico Dondo (URU) 63 75 76(9); Martín Vilarrubi (URU) d. Pablo Gonzalez (COL) 63 75 46 63.

Netherlands Antilles and Colombia relegated to Americas Zone Group III in 2004

RESULTS

Asia/Oceania Zone
First Round 7-9 February

Lebanon defeated Iran 3-2, Tehran IRI; Clay (I): Ashkan Shokoofi (IRI) d. Hicham Zaatini (LIB) 36 63 64 61; Patrick Chucri (LIB) d. Akbar Taheri (IRI) 75 63 61; Patrick Chucri/Hicham Zaatini (LIB) d. Ashkan Shokoofi/Akbar Taheri (IRI) 75 63 76(4); Anoosha Shahgholi (IRI) d. Hicham Zaatini (LIB) 16 64 63 36 61; Patrick Chucri (LIB) d. Ashkan Shokoofi (IRI) 64 57 64 16 75.

China Hong Kong defeated Tajikistan 4-1, Hong Kong HKG; Hard (O): Asif Ismail (HKG) d. Dilshod Sharifi (TJK) 60 60 63; Hiu-Tung Yu (HKG) d. Sergei Makashin (TJK) 57 62 64 63; John Hui/Asif Ismail (HKG) d. Sergei Makashin/Dilshod Sharifi (TJK) 61 61 62; Sergei Makashin (TJK) d. Asif Ismail (HKG) 76(4) 26 76(5); Hiu-Tung Yu (HKG) d. Dilshod Sharifi (TJK) 61 61.

Chinese Taipei defeated Kazakhstan 4-1, Taiwan TPE; Carpet (I): Yen-Hsun Lu (TPE) d. Dias Doskarayev (KAZ) 75 60 75; Yeu-Tzuoo Wang (TPE) d. Alexey Kedriouk (KAZ) 64 61 62; Yen-Hsun Lu/Yeu-Tzuoo Wang (TPE) d. Dias Doskarayev/Alexey Kedriouk (KAZ) 61 61 61; Alexey Kedriouk (KAZ) d. Ti Chen (TPE) 63 61; Wei-Jen Cheng (TPE) d. Anton Tsymbalov (KAZ) 63 60.

China defeated Philippines 3-0 Hankou CHN; Hard (O): Shao-Xuan Zeng (CHN) d. Johnny Arcilla (PHI) 62 61 63; Ben-Qiang Zhu (CHN) d. Joseph Victorino (PHI) 60 60 61; Ran Xu/Shao-Xuan Zeng (CHN) d. Johnny Arcilla/Michael Mora (PHI) 62 61 63; final two rubbers abandoned.

Second Round 4-6 April

Chinese Taipei defeated China, P.R. 3-2, Wuhan CHN; Hard (O): Yen-Hsun Lu (TPE) d. Peng Sun (CHN) 64 63 46 57 64; Ben-Qiang Zhu (CHN) d. Yeu-Tzuoo Wang (TPE) 76(2) 67(8) 61 61; Yen-Hsun Lu/Yeu-Tzuoo Wang (TPE) d. Ran Xu/Shao-Xuan Zeng (CHN) 46 64 60 63; Ben-Qiang Zhu (CHN) d. Yen-Hsun Lu (TPE) 62 61 ret; Yeu-Tzuoo Wang (TPE) d. Shao-Xuan Zeng (CHN) 63 64 62.

China Hong Kong defeated Lebanon 3-1 (rescheduled for 20-22 June), Colombo SRI; Hard (O): Patrick Chucri (LIB) d. Hiu-Tung Yu (HKG) 62 16 64 30 ret; Wayne Wong (HKG) d. Karim Alayli (LIB) 61 16 75 63; Brian Hung/Ling Lu (HKG) d. Karim Alayli/Patrick Chucri (LIB) 61 63 64; Wayne Wong (HKG) d. Patrick Chucri (LIB) 57 36 75 64 63; Hiu-Tung Yu (HKG) vs. Karim Alayli (LIB) - not played.

Third Round 11-13 July

Chinese Taipei defeated China Hong Kong 4-1, Kaohsiung, TPE; Hard (O): Yeu-Tzuoo Wang (TPE) d. Hiu-Tung Yu (HKG) 60 64 61; Yen-Hsun Lu (TPE) d. Wayne Wong (HKG) 64 61 63; Yen-Hsun Lu/Yeu-Tzuoo Wang (TPE) d. John Hui/Brian Hung (HKG) 63 62 64; Ti Chen (TPE) d. Hiu-Tung Yu (HKG) 64 60; Wayne Wong (HKG) d. Wei-Jen Cheng (TPE) 61 62.

Chinese Taipei promoted to Asia/Oceania Zone Group I in 2004

Play-off 4-6 April

Iran defeated Tajikistan 5-0, Dushanbe TJK; Clay (O): Anoosha Shahgholi (IRI) d. Mansour Yakhyaev (TJK) 57 76(4) 63 64; Ashkan Shokoofi (IRI) d. Sergei Makashin (TJK) 76(1) 16 64 63; Anoosha Shahgholi/Akbar Taheri (IRI) d. Sergei Makashin/Mansour Yakhyaev (TJK) 36 63 75 26 64; Shahab Hassani-Nafez (IRI) d. Dilshod Sharifi (TJK) 63 63; Ashkan Shokoofi (IRI) d. Aziz Avganov (TJK) 64 61.

Philippines defeated Kazakhstan 3-2, Manila PHI; Clay (I): Joseph Victorino (PHI) d. Anton Tsymbalov (KAZ) 64 64 64; Johnny Arcilla (PHI) d. Alexey Kedriouk (KAZ) 36 46 62 75 62; Johnny Arcilla/Michael Mora (PHI) d. Alexey Kedriouk/Anton Tsymbalov (KAZ) 46 75 63 57 64; Alexey Kedriouk (KAZ) d. Joseph Victorino (PHI) 75 76(7); Anton Tsymbalov (KAZ) d. Rolando Jr. Ruel (PHI) 62 63

Tajikistan and Kazakhstan relegated to Asia/Oceania Zone Group III in 2004

GROUP III
Euro/African Zone – Venue I

Date: 3-7 February **Venue:** Algiers, Algeria **Surface:** Clay (O)
Group A: Estonia, Hungary, Madagascar, Namibia
Group B: Algeria, Angola, Armenia, Lithuania

Group A

3 February Hungary defeated Estonia 3-0: Gergely Kisgyorgy (HUN) d. Andrei Luzgin (EST) 62 61; Kornel Bardoczky (HUN) d. Mait Kunnap (EST) 63 61; Laszlo Fono/Sebo Kiss (HUN) d. Mait Kunnap/Gert Vilms (EST) 46 64 119.

Madagascar defeated Namibia 3-0: Lalaina Ratsimbazafy (MAD) d. Henrico Du Plessis (NAM) 46 76(4) 62; Donne-Dubert Radison (MAD) d. Jean-Pierre Huish (NAM) 62 62; Donne-Dubert Radison/Jean-Marc Randriamanalina (MAD) d. Nicky Buys/Henrico Du Plessis (NAM) 36 63 62.

4 February Hungary defeated Madagascar 3-0: Gergely Kisgyorgy (HUN) d. Lalaina Ratsimbazafy (MAD) 62 62; Kornel Bardoczky (HUN) d. Donne-Dubert Radison (MAD) 60 75; Laszlo Fono/Sebo Kiss (HUN) d. Donne-Dubert Radison/Lalaina Ratsimbazafy (MAD) 62 60.

Estonia defeated Namibia 3-0: Mait Kunnap (EST) d. Henrico Du Plessis (NAM) 61 62; Gert Vilms (EST) d. Jean-Pierre Huish (NAM) 62 62; Mait Kunnap/Andrei Luzgin (EST) d. Jean-Pierre Huish/Jurgens Strydom (NAM) 63 46 63.

5 February Hungary defeated Namibia 3-0: Gergely Kisgyorgy (HUN) d. Nicky Buys (NAM) 60 60; Kornel Bardoczky (HUN) d. Jean-Pierre Huish (NAM) 61 61; Laszlo Fono/Sebo Kiss (HUN) d. Nicky Buys/Jurgens Strydom (NAM) 60 63.

Estonia defeated Madagascar 3-0: Andrei Luzgin (EST) d. Lalaina Ratsimbazafy (MAD) 75 76(1); Gert Vilms (EST) d. Donne-Dubert Radison (MAD) 63 75; Mait Kunnap/Andrei Luzgin (EST) d. Jean-Marc Randriamanalina/Lalaina Ratsimbazafy (MAD) 61 61.

Group B

3 February Lithuania defeated Armenia 3-0: Aivaras Balzekas (LTU) d. Hayk Hakobyan (ARM) 63 63; Rolandos Murashka (LTU) d. Hayk Zohranyan (ARM) 61 60; Aivaras Balzekas/Rolandos Murashka (LTU) d. Hayk Hakobyan/Hayk Zohranyan (ARM) 62 62.

Algeria defeated Angola 3-0: Abdel-Hak Hameurlaine (ALG) d. Nelson De Almeida (ANG) 75 75; Lamine Ouahab (ALG) d. Jose Nenganga (ANG) 61 61; Noureddine Mahmoudi/Lamine Ouahab (ALG) d. Joao-Sebastiao Miguel/Jose Nenganga (ANG) 62 61.

4 February Armenia defeated Algeria 3-0: Noureddine Mahmoudi (ALG) d. Hayk Hakobyan (ARM) 62 62; Abdel-Hak Hameurlaine (ALG) d. Hayk Zohranyan (ARM) 61 63; Sofiane Dob/Lamine Ouahab (ALG) d. Hayk Hakobyan/Hayk Zohranyan (ARM) 64 62.

Lithuania defeated Angola 2-1: Aivaras Balzekas (LTU) d. Nelson De Almeida (ANG) 76(7) 63; Rolandos Murashka (LTU) d. Jose Nenganga (ANG) 61 63; Nelson De Almeida/Jose Nenganga (ANG) d. Aurimas Karpavicius/Gvidas Sabeckis (LTU) 62 26 63.

5 February Angola defeated Armenia 2-1: Nelson De Almeida (ANG) d. Hayk Hakobyan (ARM) 75 06 86; Hayk Zohranyan (ARM) d. Jose Nenganga (ANG) 75 75; Nelson De Almeida/Jose Nenganga (ANG) d. Hayk Hakobyan/Hayk Zohranyan (ARM) 46 64 63.

Algeria defeated Lithuania 2-1: Abdel-Hak Hameurlaine (ALG) d. Aivaras Balzekas (LTU) 16 63 97; Lamine Ouahab (ALG) d. Rolandos Murashka (LTU) 61 62; Rolandos Murashka/Gvidas Sabeckis (LTU) d. Sofiane Dob/Noureddine Mahmoudi (ALG) 63 62.

Play-off for 1st-4th Positions:

Results carried forward: **Hungary defeated Estonia 3-0; Algeria defeated Lithuania 2-1**

6 February Hungary defeated Lithuania 3-0: Gergely Kisgyorgy (HUN) d. Aivaras Balzekas (LTU) 62 62; Kornel Bardoczky (HUN) d. Rolandos Murashka (LTU) 62 63; Laszlo Fono/Sebo Kiss (HUN) d. Rolandos Murashka/Gvidas Sabeckis (LTU) 61 62.

Algeria defeated Estonia 2-1: Mait Kunnap (EST) d. Abdel-Hak Hameurlaine (ALG) 62 61; Lamine Ouahab (ALG) d. Gert Vilms (EST) 64 60; Noureddine Mahmoudi/Lamine Ouahab (ALG) d. Mait Kunnap/Gert Vilms (EST) 75 63.

7 February Algeria defeated Hungary 2-0: Noureddine Mahmoudi (ALG) d. Sebo Kiss (HUN) 16 75 63; Lamine Ouahab (ALG) d. Laszlo Fono (HUN) 75 63; Noureddine Mahmoudi/Lamine Ouahab (ALG) vs. Laszlo Fono/Sebo Kiss (HUN) not played.

Estonia defeated Lithuania 2-1: Andrei Luzgin (EST) d. Aurimas Karpavicius (LTU) 16 76(5) 62; Rolandos Murashka (LTU) d. Mait Kunnap (EST) 60 64; Mait Kunnap/Andrei Luzgin (EST) d. Rolandos Murashka/Gvidas Sabeckis (LTU) 63 46 64.

Play-off for 5th-8th Positions:

Results carried forward: **Madagascar defeated Namibia 3-0; Angola defeated Armenia 2-1**

6 February Madagascar defeated Armenia 2-1: Tsolak Gevorgyan (ARM) d. Lalaina Ratsimbazafy (MAD) 36 62 63; Donne-Dubert Radison (MAD) d. Hayk Zohranyan (ARM) 62 60; Donne-Dubert Radison/Lalaina Ratsimbazafy (MAD) d. Tsolak Gevorgyan/Hayk Hakobyan (ARM) 63 57 86.

Namibia defeated Angola 2-1: Nelson De Almeida (ANG) d. Henrico Du Plessis (NAM) 63 63; Jean-Pierre Huish (NAM) d. Jose Nenganga (ANG) 76(6) 57 63; Henrico Du Plessis/Jean-Pierre Huish (NAM) d. Nelson De Almeida/Jose Nenganga (ANG) 63 61.

7 February Angola defeated Madagascar 2-1: Lalaina Ratsimbazafy (MAD) d. Joao-Sebastiao Miguel (ANG) 62 63; Nelson De Almeida (ANG) d. Donne-Dubert Radison (MAD) 63 64; Nelson De Almeida/Jose Nenganga (ANG) d. Donne-Dubert Radison/Lalaina Ratsimbazafy (MAD) 36 63 97.

Namibia defeated Armenia 3-0: Henrico Du Plessis (NAM) d. Hayk Hakobyan (ARM) 62 16 61; Jean-Pierre Huish (NAM) d. Tsolak Gevorgyan (ARM) 61 16 63; Henrico Du Plessis/Jean-Pierre Huish (NAM) d. Tsolak Gevorgyan/Hayk Hakobyan (ARM) w/o.

Final Positions: 1. Algeria, 2. Hungary, 3. Estonia, 4. Lithuania, 5. Madagascar, 6. Namibia, 7. Angola, 8. Armenia.

Algeria and Hungary promoted to Europe/Africa Zone Group II in 2004
Angola and Armenia relegated to Europe/Africa Zone Group IV in 2004

Euro/African Group III - Venue II

Date: 11-15 June **Venue:** Jurmala, Latvia **Surface:** Clay (O)
Group A: Azerbaijan, Latvia, Macedonia, Moldova
Group B: Bosnia & Herzegovina, Cyprus, Georgia, Turkey

Group A

11 June Latvia defeated Moldova 2-1: Andis Juska (LAT) d. Andrei Ciumac (MDA) 46 62 61; Andrei Gorban (MDA) d. Deniss Pavlovs (LAT) 76(6) 46 86; Andris Filimonovs/Andis Juska (LAT) d. Sergeu Cuptov/Andrei Gorban (MDA) 62 64.

Azerbaijan defeated FYR of Macedonia. 2-1: Zoran Sevcenko (MKD) d. Farid Shirinov (AZE) 61 46 64; Emin Agaev (AZE) d. Predrag Rusevski (MKD) 26 61 86; Emin Agaev/Farid Shirinov (AZE) d. Predrag Rusevski/Zoran Sevcenko (MKD) 63 75

12 June FYR of Macedonia. defeated Moldova 2-1: Predrag Rusevski (MKD) d. Andrei Ciumac (MDA) 46 60 62; Andrei Gorban (MDA) d. Kristijan Mitrovski (MKD) 62 62; Predrag Rusevski/Zoran Sevcenko (MKD) d. Andrei Gorban/Denis Molcianov (MDA) 76(6) 62.

Latvia defeated Azerbaijan 2-1: Andis Juska (LAT) d. Farid Shirinov (AZE) 61 62; Emin Agaev (AZE) d. Nikita Svacko (LAT) 63 63; Andris Filimonovs/Andis Juska (LAT) d. Emin Agaev/Farid Shirinov (AZE) 64 64.

13 June Azerbaijan defeated Moldova 2-1: Denis Molcianov (MDA) d. Talat Rahimov (AZE) 60 62; Emin Agaev (AZE) d. Andrei Gorban (MDA) 67(3) 64 61; Emin Agaev/Farid Shirinov (AZE) d. Andrei Ciumac/Andrei Gorban (MDA) 64 62.

Latvia defeated FYR of Macedonia. 3-0: Andis Juska (LAT) d. Zoran Sevcenko (MKD) 64 61; Deniss Pavlovs (LAT) d. Predrag Rusevski (MKD) 64 62; Andris Filimonovs/Nikita Svacko (LAT) d. Dimitar Grabulovski/Kristijan Mitrovski (MKD) 61 62.

Group B

11 June Georgia defeated Bosnia & Herzegovina 3-0: Irakli Ushangishvili (GEO) d. Zlatan Kadric (BIH) 64 62; Irakli Labadze (GEO) d. Igor Racic (BIH) 62 63; Irakli Labadze/Irakli Ushangishvili (GEO) d. Ivan Dodig/Zlatan Kadric (BIH) 63 61.

Cyprus defeated Turkey 3-0: Fotos Kallias (CYP) d. Ergun Zorlu (TUR) 26 64 97; Marcos Baghdatis (CYP) d. Haluk Akkoyun (TUR) 63 60; Marcos Baghdatis/Dinos Pavlou (CYP) d. Doruk Baglan/Ergun Zorlu (TUR) 62 63.

12 June Georgia defeated Turkey 2-1: Irakli Ushangishvili (GEO) d. Ergun Zorlu (TUR) 46 76(7) 75; Irakli Labadze (GEO) d. Haluk Akkoyun (TUR) 62 61; Haluk Akkoyun/Esat Tanik (TUR) d. David Kvernadze/Omari Murgulia (GEO) 60 62.

Cyprus defeated Bosnia & Herzegovina 3-0: Fotos Kallias (CYP) d. Ivan Dodig (BIH) 62 61; Marcos Baghdatis (CYP) d. Igor Racic (BIH) 61 63; Marcos Baghdatis/Dinos Pavlou (CYP) d. Ivan Dodig/Zlatan Kadric (BIH) 75 63.

13 June Georgia defeated Cyprus 2-1: Fotos Kallias (CYP) d. Irakli Ushangishvili (GEO) 62 16 62; Irakli Labadze (GEO) d. Marcos Baghdatis (CYP) 36 63 64; Irakli Labadze/Irakli Ushangishvili (GEO) d. Marcos Baghdatis/Dinos Pavlou (CYP) 76(3) 75.

Turkey defeated Bosni & Herzegovina 2-1: Ergun Zorlu (TUR) d. Haris Basalic (BIH) 64 62; Igor Racic (BIH) d. Haluk Akkoyun (TUR) 62 76(3); Haluk Akkoyun/Ergun Zorlu (TUR) d. Ivan Dodig/Igor Racic (BIH) 60 63.

Play-off for 1st-4th Positions:

Results carried forward: **Georgia defeated Cyprus 2-1; Latvia defeated Azerbaijan 2-1**

14 June Georgia defeated Azerbaijan 3-0: Irakli Ushangishvili (GEO) d. Farid Shirinov (AZE) 75 62; Irakli Labadze (GEO) d. Emin Agaev (AZE) 1-0 ret; Irakli Labadze/Irakli Ushangishvili (GEO) d. Fakhreddin Shirinov/Farid Shirinov (AZE) 61 61.

Latvia defeated Cyprus 2-1: Andis Juska (LAT) d. Fotos Kallias (CYP) 76(10) 62; Marcos Baghdatis (CYP) d. Nikita Svacko (LAT) 61 61; Andris Filimonovs/Andis Juska (LAT) d. Marcos Baghdatis/Dinos Pavlou (CYP) 62 36 63.

15 June Georgia defeated Latvia 2-1: Irakli Ushangishvili (GEO) d. Andis Juska (LAT) 63 67(5) 64; Irakli Labadze (GEO) d. Nikita Svacko (LAT) 62 64; Andris Filimonovs/Nikita Svacko (LAT) d. David Kvernadze/Omari Murgulia (GEO) 63 63.

Cyprus defeated Azerbaijan 3-0: Fotos Kallias (CYP) d. Farid Shirinov (AZE) 61 61; Marcos Baghdatis (CYP) d. Fakhreddin Shirinov (AZE) 62 62; Eleftherios Christou/Dinos Pavlou (CYP) d. Talat Rahimov/Farid Shirinov (AZE) 63 61.

Play-off for 5th-8th Positions:

Results carried forward: **Turkey defeated Bosnia & Herzegovinia 2-1; FYR of Macedonia defeated Moldova 2-1**

14 June Turkey defeated FYR of Macedonia 2-1: Predrag Rusevski (MKD) d. Esat Tanik (TUR) 36 62 61; Haluk Akkoyun (TUR) d. Kristijan Mitrovski (MKD) 63 62; Haluk Akkoyun/Esat Tanik (TUR) d. Predrag Rusevski/Zoran Sevcenko (MKD) 63 64.

Moldova defeated Bosnia & Herzegovina 3-0: Andrei Ciumac (MDA) d. Zlatan Kadric (BIH) 26 75 64; Andrei Gorban (MDA) d. Igor Racic (BIH) 76(10) 64; Sergeu Cuptov/Andrei Gorban (MDA) d. Ivan Dodig/Zlatan Kadric (BIH) 63 75.

15 June Turkey defeated Moldova 2-0: Esat Tanik (TUR) d. Denis Molcianov (MDA) 61 26 1412; Haluk Akkoyun (TUR) d. Andrei Gorban (MDA) 64 36 62; Haluk Akkoyun/Esat Tanik (TUR) vs. Andrei Gorban/Denis Molcianov (MDA) - not played.

FYR of Macedonia. defeated Bosnia/Herzegovina 3-0: Predrag Rusevski (MKD) d. Ivan Dodig (BIH) 75 61; Dimitar Grabulovski (MKD) d. Zlatan Kadric (BIH) 64 76(3); Dimitar Grabulovski/Kristijan Mitrovski (MKD) d. Ivan Dodig/Zlatan Kadric (BIH) 64 64.

Final Positions: 1. Georgia, 2. Latvia, 3. Cyprus, 4. Azerbaijan, 5. Turkey, 6. FYR of Macedonia, 7. Moldova, 8. Bosnia & Herzegovina.

Georgia and Latvia promoted to Europe/Africa Zone Group II in 2004
Moldova and Bosnia & Herzegovina relegated to Europe/Africa Zone Group IV in 2004

RESULTS

Play-off for 5th-7th Positions:

Results carried forward: **Zambia defeated Mauritius 2-1**

14 June Malta defeated Zambia 3-0: Marcus Delicata (MLT) d. Mwiza Gondwe (ZAM) 60 64; Mark Schembri (MLT) d. Edgar Kazembe (ZAM) 63 60; Marcus Delicata/Mark Schembri (MLT) d. Mwiza Gondwe/Hector Sando (ZAM) 61 62.

15 June Malta defeated Mauritius 2-1: Alexandre Daruty (MRI) d. Marcus Delicata (MLT) 63 64; Mark Schembri (MLT) d. Simon Koenig (MRI) 75 64; Marcus Delicata/Mark Schembri (MLT) d. Alexandre Daruty/Abdullah Toorawa (MRI) 62 76(6).

Final Positions: 1. Iceland, 2. Kenya, 3. San Marino, 4. Rwanda, 5. Malta, 6. Zambia, 7. Mauritius.

Iceland and Kenya promoted to Europe/Africa Zone Group III in 2004

Euro/African Zone - Venue II

Date: 5-9 February **Venue:** Lagos, Nigeria **Surface:** Hard (O)
Group A: Botswana, Burkina Faso, Djibouti, Mali, Togo
Group B: Benin, Gabon, Nigeria, Senegal, Uganda

Group A

5 February Botswana defeated Djibouti 3-0: Keneilwe Phuthego (BOT) d. Abdo-Ali Abdallah (DJI) 60 60; Thato Kgosimore (BOT) d. Kadar Mogueh (DJI) 60 61; Phenyo Matong/Modisaotsile Phatshwane (BOT) d. Abdi-Fatah Abolourahman Youssouf/Kadar Mogueh (DJI) 62 61.

Togo defeated Burkina Faso 3-0: Jean-Kome Loglo (TOG) d. Mamadou Kabore (BUR) 64 60; Komlavi Loglo (TOG) d. Sansan Dabire (BUR) 63 36 63; Kwami Gakpo/Jean-Kome Loglo (TOG) d. Mamadou Kabore/Kader Nanema (BUR) 64 61.

6 February Togo defeated Djibouti 3-0: Komlavi Loglo (TOG) d. Abdi-Fatah Abolourahman Youssouf (DJI) 60 60; Kwami Gakpo (TOG) d. Abdo-Ali Abdallah (DJI) 60 60; Kwami Gakpo/Komlavi Loglo (TOG) d. Kadar Mogueh/Isse Willo (DJI) 60 60.

Burkina Faso defeated Mali 3-0: Kader Nanema (BUR) d. Madou Keita (MLI) 75 62; Sansan Dabire (BUR) d. Amadou Diallo (MLI) 62 63; Sansan Dabire/Mamadou Kabore (BUR) d. Amadou Diallo/Madou Keita (MLI) 64 62.

7 February Burkina Faso defeated Botswana 2-1: Thato Kgosimore (BOT) d. Mamadou Kabore (BUR) 46 64 63; Sansan Dabire (BUR) d. Modisaotsile Phatshwane (BOT) 64 60; Sansan Dabire/Mamadou Kabore (BUR) d. Thato Kgosimore/Keneilwe Phuthego (BOT) 64 36 64.

Togo defeated Mali 3-0: Komlavi Loglo (TOG) d. Madou Keita (MLI) 60 60; Jean-Kome Loglo (TOG) d. Yaya Traore (MLI) 61 75; Kwami Gakpo/Jean-Kome Loglo (TOG) d. Amadou Diallo/Yaya Traore (MLI) 60 62.

8 February Botswana defeated Mali 2-1: Keneilwe Phuthego (BOT) d. Yaya Traore (MLI) 61 36 61; Thato Kgosimore (BOT) d. Amadou Diallo (MLI) 61 62; Amadou Diallo/Yaya Traore (MLI) d. Phenyo Matong/Modisaotsile Phatshwane (BOT) 62 75.

Burkina Faso defeated Djibouti 3-0: Kader Nanema (BUR) d. Isse Willo (DJI) 60 60; Mamadou Kabore (BUR) d. Kadar Mogueh (DJI) 62 60; Mamadou Kabore/Kader Nanema (BUR) d. Abdo-Ali Abdallah/Isse Willo (DJI) 60 60.

9 February Togo defeated Botswana 3-0: Jean-Kome Loglo (TOG) d. Keneilwe Phuthego (BOT) 64 63; Komlavi Loglo (TOG) d. Thato Kgosimore (BOT) 64 60; Kwami Gakpo/Jean-Kome Loglo (TOG) d. Modisaotsile Phatshwane/Keneilwe Phuthego (BOT) 64 62.

Mali defeated Djibouti 3-0: Madou Keita (MLI) d. Abdi-Fatah Abolourahman Youssouf (DJI) 60 61; Amadou Diallo (MLI) d. Abdo-Ali Abdallah (DJI) 63 60; Madou Keita/Yaya Traore (MLI) d. Abdo-Ali Abdallah/Abdi-Fatah Abolourahman Youssouf (DJI) 60 60.

Final Positions: 1. Togo, 2. Burkina Faso, 3. Botswana, 4. Mali, 5. Djibouti.

Group B

5 February Nigeria defeated Gabon 3-0: Jonathan Igbinovia (NGR) d. Joseph-Patrick Oyone-Meye (GAB) 62 62; Abdul-Mumin Babalola (NGR) d. Christophe Couprie (GAB) 61 61; Abdul-Mumin Babalola/Jonathan Igbinovia (NGR) d. Didier Momo-Kassa/Joseph-Patrick Oyone-Meye (GAB) 62 62.

Benin defeated Uganda 3-0: Christophe Pognon (BEN) d. Patrick Olobo (UGA) 61 61; Arnaud Segodo (BEN) d. Charles Yokwe (UGA) 64 60; Armand Segodo/Rodrigue Vignikin (BEN) d. Patrick Ochan/Charles Yokwe (UGA) 61 57 75.

6 February Benin defeated Gabon 3-0: Christophe Pognon (BEN) d. Joseph-Patrick Oyone-Meye (GAB) 62 61; Arnaud Segodo (BEN) d. Christophe Couprie (GAB) 61 43 ret; Armand Segodo/Rodrique Vignikin (BEN) d. Yvan Mefane/Didier Momo-Kassa (GAB) 63 63.

Senegal defeated Uganda 3-0: Daouda Ndiaye (SEN) d. Ronald Semanda (UGA) 62 75; Djadji Ka (SEN) d. Patrick Ochan (UGA) 62 62; Djadji Ka/Daouda Ndiaye (SEN) d. Patrick Ochan/Charles Yokwe (UGA) 62 62.

7 February Nigeria defeated Uganda 3-0: Jonathan Igbinovia (NGR) d. Ronald Semanda (UGA) 61 60; Sunday Jegede (NGR) d. Patrick Olobo (UGA) 64 46 61; Toyin Dairo/Jonathan Igbinovia (NGR) d. Patrick Ochan/Patrick Olobo (UGA) 61 61.

Benin defeated Senegal 2-1: Christophe Pognon (BEN) d. Daouda Ndiaye (SEN) 63 62; Arnaud Segodo (BEN) d. Djadji Ka (SEN) 75 63; Djadji Ka/Daouda Ndiaye (SEN) d. Armand Segodo/Rodrique Vignikin (BEN) 16 76(7) 64.

8 February Nigeria defeated Senegal 3-0: Jonathan Igbinovia (NGR) d. Daouda Ndiaye (SEN) 63 76(2); Abdul-Mumin Babalola (NGR) d. Djadji Ka (SEN) 61 63; Toyin Dairo/Jonathan Igbinovia (NGR) d. Djadji Ka/Daouda Ndiaye (SEN) 62 63.

Gabon defeated Uganda 3-0: Joseph-Patrick Oyone-Meye (GAB) d. Patrick Olobo (UGA) 76(2) 63; Christophe Couprie (GAB) d. Charles Yokwe (UGA) 60 64; Christophe Couprie/Joseph-Patrick Oyone-Meye (GAB) d. Patrick Olobo/Charles Yokwe (UGA) 63 75.

9 February Benin defeated Nigeria 2-1: Jonathan Igbinovia (NGR) d. Christophe Pognon (BEN) 63 76(5); Arnaud Segodo (BEN) d. Abdul-Mumin Babalola (NGR) 63 62; Christophe Pognon/Arnaud Segodo (BEN) d. Toyin Dairo/Jonathan Igbinovia (NGR) 36 76(6) 75.

Gabon defeated Senegal 2-1: Joseph-Patrick Oyone-Meye (GAB) d. Youssou Berthe (SEN) 62 46 64; Christophe Couprie (GAB) d. Djadji Ka (SEN) 57 62 61; Djadji Ka/Daouda Ndiaye (SEN) d. Yvan Mefane/Didier Momo-Kassa (GAB) 62 62.

Final Positions: 1. Benin, 2. Nigeria, 3. Gabon, 4. Senegal, 5. Uganda.

Benin and Togo promoted to Europe/Africa Zone Group III in 2004

American Zone

Date: 31 March - 6 April **Venue:** San Jose, Costa Rica **Surface:** Hard (O)
Nations: Costa Rica, Bermuda, Barbados, Eastern Caribbean, Panama, US Virgin Islands

31 March US Virgin Islands defeated Costa Rica 2-1: Kenny Callendar (ISV) d. David Alvarado (CRC) 36 64 61; Eugene Highfield (ISV) d. Juan-Carlos Gonzalez (CRC) 46 76(6) 61; Diego Alvarado/Marck Van Der Laat-Robles (CRC) d. Nicholas Bass/John Richards (ISV) 36 76(7) 64.

Panama defeated Eastern Caribbean 3-0: Alberto Gonzalez (PAN) d. Glynn James (ECA) 62 64; Chad Valdez (PAN) d. Kirt Cable (ECA) 62 61; Abad Goon/David Lopez (PAN) d. Deron Grant/Trevor Sam (ECA) 62 62.

Barbados defeated Bermuda 2-1: Duane Williams (BAR) d. Janson Bascome (BER) 61 36 61; James Collieson (BER) d. Damien Applewhaite (BAR) 64 61; Akil Burgess/Michael Date (BAR) d. Janson Bascome/Richard Mallory (BER) 64 36 63.

1 April Costa Rica defeated Eastern Caribbean 2-1: David Alvarado (CRC) d. Glynn James (ECA) 76(2) 64; Juan-Carlos Gonzalez (CRC) d. Kirt Cable (ECA) 64 63; Kirt Cable/Glynn James (ECA) d. Diego Alvarado/Marck Van Der Laat-Robles (CRC) 62 61.

Bermuda defeated Panama 2-1: Janson Bascome (BER) d. Alberto Gonzalez (PAN) 46 64 62; Chad Valdez (PAN) d. James Collieson (BER) 36 62 61; Janson Bascome/James Collieson (BER) d. Abad Goon/Chad Valdez (PAN) 46 75 63.

US Virgin Islands defeated Barbados 2-1: Kenny Callendar (ISV) d. Duane Williams (BAR) 75 36 64; Eugene Highfield (ISV) d. Damien Applewhaite (BAR) 61 61; Akil Burgess/Michael Date (BAR) d. Nicholas Bass/John Richards (ISV) 36 62 64.

2 April Costa Rica defeated Barbados 2-1: David Alvarado (CRC) d. Akil Burgess (BAR) 62 36 64; Juan-Carlos Gonzalez (CRC) d. Duane Williams (BAR) 63 61; Damien Applewhaite/Michael Date (BAR) d. Diego Alvarado/Marck Van Der Laat-Robles (CRC) 62 64.

RESULTS

Panama defeated US Virgin Islands 3-0: Alberto Gonzalez (PAN) d. Kenny Callendar (ISV) 64 06 75; Chad Valdez (PAN) d. Eugene Highfield (ISV) 36 64 62; Abad Goon/David Lopez (PAN) d. Nicholas Bass/John Richards (ISV) 63 62.

Bermuda defeated Eastern Caribbean 3-0: Janson Bascome (BER) d. Glynn James (ECA) 60 62; James Collieson (BER) d. Kirt Cable (ECA) 61 67(5) 64; Richard Mallory/Jovan Whitter (BER) d. Kirt Cable/Deron Grant (ECA) 75 64.

4 April Costa Rica defeated Bermuda 3-0: David Alvarado (CRC) d. Janson Bascome (BER) 76(9) 61; Juan-Carlos Gonzalez (CRC) d. James Collieson (BER) 62 62; Diego Alvarado/Marck Van Der Laat-Robles (CRC) d. Richard Mallory/Jovan Whitter (BER) 64 64.

Panama defeated Barbados 2-1: Alberto Gonzalez (PAN) d. Akil Burgess (BAR) 36 76(3) 86; Chad Valdez (PAN) d. Duane Williams (BAR) 46 63 75; Damien Applewhaite/Michael Date (BAR) d. Abad Goon/David Lopez (PAN) 63 36 97.

US Virgin Islands defeated Eastern Caribbean 3-0: Kenny Callendar (ISV) d. Deron Grant (ECA) 62 60; Eugene Highfield (ISV) d. Kirt Cable (ECA) 76(3) 61; . Nicholas Bass/John Richards (ISV) d. Deron Grant/Glynn James (ECA) 63 67(5) 64.

5 April Panama defeated Costa Rica 2-1: David Alvarado (CRC) d. Alberto Gonzalez (PAN) 64 76(2); Chad Valdez (PAN) d. Juan-Carlos Gonzalez (CRC) 62 36 62; Abad Goon/David Lopez (PAN) d. Diego Alvarado/Juan-Carlos Gonzalez (CRC) 26 63 64.

US Virgin Islands defeated Bermuda 2-1: Kenny Callendar (ISV) d. Janson Bascome (BER) 63 76(3); Eugene Highfield (ISV) d. James Collieson (BER) 63 60; Richard Mallory/Jovan Whitter (BER) d. Nicholas Bass/John Richards (ISV) 46 64 63.

Barbados defeated Eastern Caribbean 3-0: Michael Date (BAR) d. Deron Grant (ECA) 76(4) 62; Damien Applewhaite (BAR) d. Kirt Cable (ECA) 63 26 75; Akil Burgess/Duane Williams (BAR) d. Deron Grant/Trevor Sam (ECA) 61 61.

Final Positions: 1. Panama, 2. US Virgin Islands, 3. Costa Rica, 4. Bermuda, 5. Barbados, 6. Eastern Caribbean.

Panama and US Virgin Islands promoted to Americas Zone Group III in 2004.

Asia/Oceania Zone

Date: 16-22 June **Venue:** Colombo, Sri Lanka **Surface:** Clay (O)
Group A: Brunei, Saudi Arabia, Sri Lanka, Vietnam
Group B: Bangladesh, Myanmar, Oman, Singapore

Group A

18 June Vietnam defeated Sri Lanka 2-1: Rohan De Silva (SRI) d. Quang-Huy Ngo (VIE) w/o; Minh-Quan Do (VIE) d. Rajeev Rajapakse (SRI) 76(2) 64; Quoc-Khanh Le/Duc-Duong Ngo (VIE) d. Rohan De Silva/Franklyn Emmanuel (SRI) 63 62.

Saudi Arabia defeated Brunei 3-0: Badar Al Megayel (KSA) d. Wong-Kee Loong (BRU) 64 63; Omar Al Thagib (KSA) d. Ismasufian Ibrahim (BRU) 61 62; Badar Al Megayel/Fahad Al Saad (KSA) d. Abdul-Rasheed Abdullah/Mohamed Ridzuan-Yunos (BRU) 61 61.

19 June Saudi Arabia defeated Sri Lanka 2-0: Badar Al Megayel (KSA) d. Franklyn Emmanuel (SRI) 76(4) 63; Omar Al Thagib (KSA) d. Harshana Godamanna (SRI) 75 64; Rohan De Silva/Rajeev Rajapakse (SRI) vs. Badar Al Megayel/Fahad Al Saad (KSA) not played.

Vietnam defeated Brunei 2-0: Quoc-Khanh Le (VIE) d. Abdul-Rasheed Abdullah (BRU) 60 30 ret; Quang-Huy Ngo (VIE) d. Wong-Kee Loong (BRU) 62 62; Quoc-Khanh Le/Duc-Duong Ngo (VIE) vs. Abdul-Rasheed Abdullah/Ismasufian Ibrahim (BRU) - not played.

20 June Sri Lanka defeated Brunei 3-0: Rajeev Rajapakse (SRI) d. Wong-Kee Loong (BRU) 61 61; Harshana Godamanna (SRI) d. Ismasufian Ibrahim (BRU) 60 61; Rohan De Silva/Rajeev Rajapakse (SRI) d. Ismasufian Ibrahim/Wong-Kee Loong (BRU) 60 61.

Vietnam defeated Saudi Arabia 2-1: Fahad Al Saad (KSA) d. Quoc-Khanh Le (VIE) 36 76(5) 64; Minh-Quan Do (VIE) d. Omar Al Thagib (KSA) 76(5) 61; Minh-Quan Do/Quoc-Khanh Le (VIE) d. Badar Al Megayel/Fahad Al Saad (KSA) 26 75 60.

Group B

18 June Singapore defeated Bangladesh 2-1: Kam-Kok Heun (SIN) d. Hira-Lal Rahman (BAN) 62 67(3) 63; Sree Roy (BAN) d. Kamil Ghazali (SIN) 61 64; Lim-Ming Chye/Heryanta Dewandaka (SIN) d. Hira-Lal Rahman/Sree Roy (BAN) 60 63.

Oman defeated Myanmar 3-0: Mohammed Al Nabhani (OMA) d. Min Min (MYA) 61 64; Khalid Al Nabhani (OMA) d. Zaw-Zaw Latt (MYA) 26 64 62; Khalid Al Nabhani/Mohammed Al Nabhani (OMA) d. Zaw-Zaw Latt/Khin-Maung Win (MYA) 62 57 97.

19 June Myanmar defeated Singapore 2-1: Khin-Maung Win (MYA) d. Kam-Kok Heun (SIN) 64 06 61; Zaw-Zaw Latt (MYA) d. Kamil Ghazali (SIN) 63 64; Lim-Ming Chye/Heryanta Dewandaka (SIN) d. Zaw-Zaw Latt/Khin-Maung Win (MYA) 64 06 64.

Oman defeated Bangladesh 2-1: Hira-Lal Rahman (BAN) d. Mohammed Al Nabhani (OMA) 75 62; Khalid Al Nabhani (OMA) d. Sree Roy (BAN) 62 61; Khalid Al Nabhani/Mohammed Al Nabhani (OMA) d. Hira-Lal Rahman/Sree Roy (BAN) 62 75.

20 June Oman defeated Singapore 2-1: Mohammed Al Nabhani (OMA) d. Kam-Kok Heun (SIN) 60 64; Khalid Al Nabhani (OMA) d. Kamil Ghazali (SIN) 61 62; Lim-Ming Chye/Heryanta Dewandaka (SIN) d. Khalid Al Nabhani/Mohammed Al Nabhani (OMA) 64 62.

Myanmar defeated Bangladesh 3-0: Khin-Maung Win (MYA) d. Hira-Lal Rahman (BAN) 62 75; Zaw-Zaw Latt (MYA) d. Sree Roy (BAN) 36 75 63; Tu Maw/Min Min (MYA) d. Abu-Hena-Tasawar Collins/Aktar Hussain (BAN) 64 62.

Play-off for 1st-4th Positions:

Results carried forward: **Vietnam defeated Saudi Arabia 2-1; Oman defeated Myanmar 3-0**

21/22 June Oman defeated Saudi Arabia 2-1: Fahad Al Saad (KSA) d. Mohammed Al Nabhani (OMA) 26 76(9) 63; Khalid Al Nabhani (OMA) d. Badar Al Megayel (KSA) 26 63 75; Khalid Al Nabhani/Mohammed Al Nabhani (OMA) d. Badar Al Megayel/Fahad Al Saad (KSA) 62 75.

Vietnam defeated Myanmar 3-0: Quang-Huy Ngo (VIE) d. Khin-Maung Win (MYA) 36 63 62; Minh-Quan Do (VIE) d. Zaw-Zaw Latt (MYA) 62 76(7); Quoc-Khanh Le/Duc-Duong Ngo (VIE) d. Zaw-Zaw Latt/Khin-Maung Win (MYA) 63 64.

Play-off for 5th-8th Positions: not played due to rain.

Final Positions: 1= Oman, Vietnam, 3= Myanmar, Saudi Arabia, 5= Bangladesh, Brunei, Singapore, Sri Lanka.

Oman and Vietnam promoted to Asia/Oceania Zone Group III in 2004

ACKNOWLEDGMENTS
and photography credits

ACKNOWLEDGMENTS

THIS IS MY FOURTH YEAR as the author of this wonderful book and for that, of course, many thanks to Barbara Travers, head of communications at the ITF, for her continued unstinting support. I am sure she would be the first, too, to acknowledge that BNP Paribas has become a highly valued sponsor and friend.

The participants have, as ever, delivered rich and fulsome color to my year and I'd like to express special gratitude to those who have given their time, be they players or captains: Karim Alami, Hicham Arazi, Jordi Arrese, Wayne Arthurs, Alex Bogdanovic, Agustin Calleri, Alex Corretja, Younes El Aynaoui, Roger Federer, Juan Carlos Ferrero, John Fitzgerald, Tim Henman, Lleyton Hewitt, Gustavo Kuerten, Feliciano Lopez, Alan Mackin, Patrick McEnroe, Carlos Moya, David Nalbandian, Mark Philippoussis, Andy Roddick, Greg Rusedski, Roger Taylor, and Todd Woodbridge.

Thanks to the head of sport at The Times, Keith Blackmore, for encouraging this venture and supporting it fully. To those in the press corps who have always been ready and willing with a quote or an initiative here and there, they know who they are. I must apologize to those smashing people at the ATP for my constant nattering in their ears: Nicola Arzani, David Massey, Rob Penner, Benito Perez-Barbadillo, and Greg Sharko always came up with the goods and the players.

To Nick Imison, the indefatigable editor, for making sure I kept to my deadlines, and his team, for expediting the book so brilliantly. Randy Walker at the USTA is a constant source of information; Heidi Cohu at the Lawn Tennis Association balanced help and expertise with becoming a mother for the first time; John Lindsay and Debbie Miller in Australia worked wonders for the final.

From the picture men for their continued brilliance, the designers, and editor Alex Tart at Universe, superb teamwork abounded. I hope they enjoyed this as much as I did.

When I needed time and space at home, love and thanks to Maureen, Elizabeth, and Kathleen.

Neil Harman, December 1, 2003.

PHOTOGRAPHY CREDITS

- Ron Angle: 26, 27, 28, 29, 61, 64, 65, 66, 67, 68, 69
- Sergio Carmona: 36, 37, 38, 39, 41, 48, 49, 51, 62/63, 70, 71, 72, 73, 74, 75, 77
- Antoine Couvercelle: 20, 21, 22
- Arne Forsell/Bildbyran: 23, 24, 25, 44, 45, 47
- Andrei Golovanov and Sergei Kivrin: 30, 31, 32
- Tommy Hindley/Professional Sport: 12/13, 14, 15, 16
- Henk Koster: 17, 18, 19, 92
- Eric Lalmand/Photo News: 82
- Rafael Lema: 84
- Sergio Llamera: 42/43, 56, 57, 59
- Susan Mullane: 78/79, 86
- Serge Philippot: 52, 53, 55
- Kittinun Rodsupan: 94
- Marcelo Ruschel: 90
- Paul Zimmer: 5, 6, 9, 10, 33, 34, 35, 88, 97, 98/99, 100, 101, 102, 103, 104, 105, 106, 107, 108, 109, 110, 111, 112, 113, 114, 115

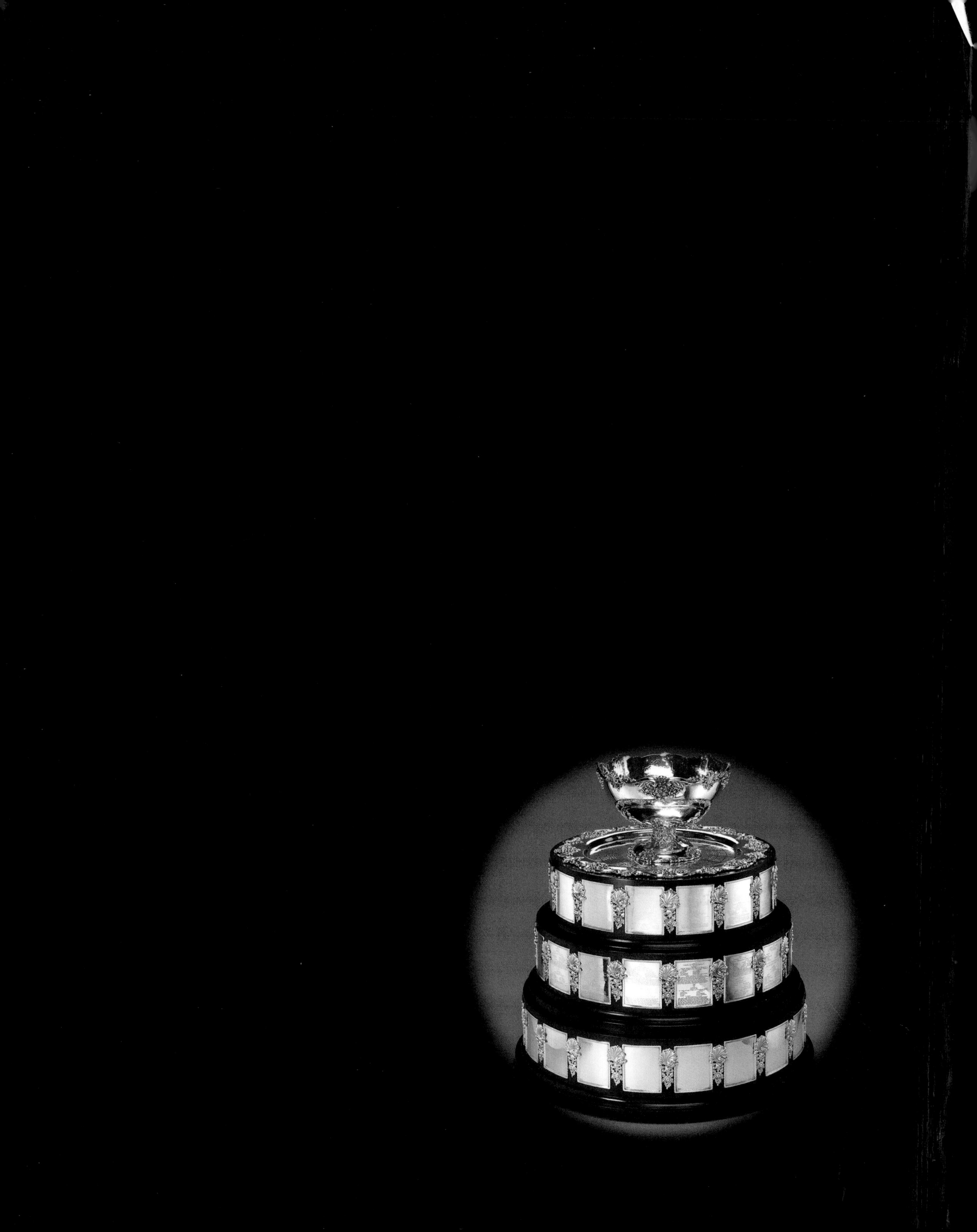

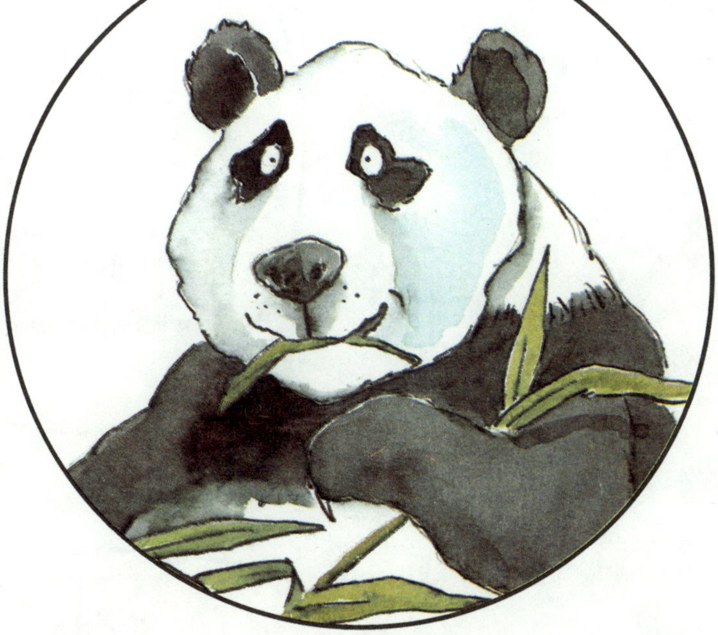

20-21
What Do Animals Eat?
- a frog eats flies
- an anteater eats ants
- a squirrel eats nuts
- a pelican eats fish
- a sheep eats grass
- a rabbit eats vegetables
- a hen eats corn
- a crow eats worms
- a panda eats bamboo
- bees eat nectar from flowers
- a dog eats meat

26-27
Baby Animals
- horse and foal
- cat and kitten
- sheep and lamb
- frog and tadpole
- goose and gosling
- cow and calf
- hen and chick
- kangaroo and joey
- dog and puppy
- lioness and lion cub

28-29
Silly Animals
- the penguin and pig should not be flying
- the sheep should have four legs, not five
- the kangaroo should be carrying a joey
- the cat should say "meow" not "baa"
- the mouse has a rabbit's tail
- the hippopotamus has an elephant's trunk
- the hen and the duck have the wrong feet
- the bee should have yellow and black stripes
- the lion should not have spots
- the parrot should not have ears
- the giraffe should not have stripes
- the cow should not have antlers
- the octopus should have eight legs, not nine
- the penguin should not be blue and pink

Answers

29

Silly Animals

What is wrong with these animals?

frog

kangaroo

lion cub

puppy

foal

lamb

kitten

chick

goose

cow

27

Baby Animals

Can you help the baby animals find their mothers?

cat

horse

sheep

tadpole

gosling

calf

hen

joey

dog

lioness

wasp nest

spiderweb

mole tunnel

bear cave

rabbit burrow

mouse hole

Animal Homes

bird nest

squirrel nest

anthills

beaver lodge

croak

squawk

roar

cluck

meow

moooo

hissssssss

Animal Sounds

neigh

woof

squeak

baaaa

quack

hee-haw

oink

22

a rabbit eats…

a hen eats…

a crow eats…

a panda eats…

bees eat…

a dog eats…

What Do Animals Eat?

a frog eats…

an anteater eats…

a squirrel eats…

a pelican eats…

a sheep eats…

mouse

guinea pig

parakeet

turtle

cat

Pets

dog

hamster

goldfish

gerbil

rabbit

cheetah

tiger

puma

jaguar

Big Cats

leopards

lynx

lion

lioness

cows

horse

ducks

bull

Farm Animals

rooster

sheep

donkey

goat

turkey

chicken

pigs

14

dolphin

fish

sea horse

starfish

octopus

Sea Animals

shark

turtle

squid

whale

lobster

eel

baboon

rhinoceros

giraffe

antelope

On Safari

elephant

ostrich

zebra

hippopotamus

flamingo

polar bear

sea lion

arctic fox

reindeer

Animals in Cold Places

penguins

walrus

seals

wolf

musk-ox

toucans

sloth

snake

butterflies

alligators

frog

Jungle Animals

howler monkeys

parrot

spider monkeys

armadillo

anteater

jaguar

hummingbird

6

18-19 Pets

20-21 What Do Animals Eat?

22-23 Animal Sounds

24-25 Animal Homes

26-27 Baby Animals

28-29 Silly Animals

30-31 Answers

CONTENTS

6-7 Jungle Animals

8-9 Animals in Cold Places

10-11 On Safari

12-13 Sea Animals

14-15 Farm Animals

16-17 Big Cats

My First Book of
ANIMALS
illustrated by
Louise Voce

Platt & Munk, Publishers • New York
A Division of Grosset & Dunlap

Copyright © 1986 by Louise Voce.
All rights reserved. First published in
the United States in 1986 by Platt & Munk,
a division of Grosset & Dunlap.
Grosset & Dunlap is a member of
The Putnam Publishing Group, New York.
Originally published in Great Britain in 1986
by Walker Books Ltd., London.
Printed in Italy.
Library of Congress Catalog Card Number: 86-80517
ISBN 0-448-10832-1 A B C D E F G H I J

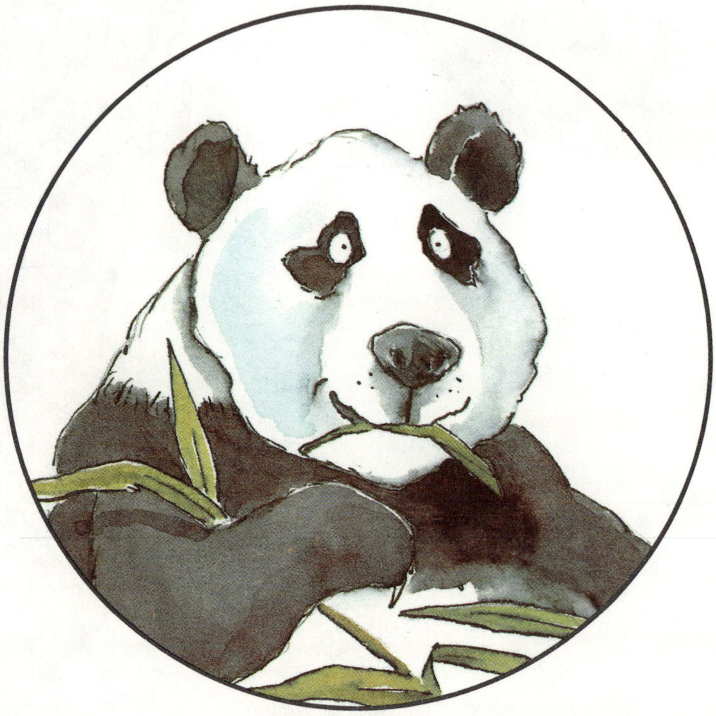